CHAMPIONSHIP VOLLEYBALL DRILLS:

Volume 1–Individual Skill Training

CHAMPIONSHIP VOLLEYBALL DRILLS:

Volume 1–Individual Skill Training

Edited by
Bob Bertucci
Ralph Hippolyte

Leisure Press
Champaign, Illinois

Leisure Press
A Division of Human Kinetics Publishers
P.O. Box 5076
Champaign, IL 61825-5076
1-800-747-4457

Canada:
Human Kinetics Publishers
Box 24040, Windsor, ON N8Y 4Y9
1-800-465-7301 (in Canada only)

Europe:
Human Kinetics Publishers (Europe) Ltd.
P.O. Box IW14, Leeds LS16 6TR, England
0532-781708

Australia:
Human Kinetics Publishers
P.O. Box 80, Kingswood 5062, South Australia
618-374-0433

New Zealand:
Human Kinetics Publishers
P.O. Box 105-231, Auckland 1
(09) 309-2259

Library of Congress Catalog Card Number: 81-86508

ISBN: 88011-034-1

Photo Credits:
Ron Hasse/Focus West: pages 30 and 94
Bruce Hazelton/Focus West: Cover and pages 42, 54, 82, and 111

10 9 8 7

CONTENTS

PREFACE

The growth of volleyball in the United States, particularly in recent years, has been phenomenal. This growth is reflected by the ever-increasing number of teams representing recreational programs, elementary schools, junior high, high schools, colleges, universities and USVBA programs.

Volleyball drills can generally be grouped into three classifications—simple, combination and complex. *Championship Volleyball Drills* is a three volume set of drills with each book devoted to one of the three classifications. The chart below illustrates the breakdown of drills into three categories.

Drill Categories

	Simple	Combination	Complex
Repetition	One repetition of one skill.	One repetition of two or more skills in a drill, not in succession.	One repetition of two or more skills performed in succession.
	Multiple repetitions of one skill in succession.	Multiple repetitions of each skill in succession, two or more skills in a drill.	Multiple repetitions of two or more skills performed in succession.

This volume addresses the category of simple drills. The importance of drills cannot be overemphasized. A coach cannot expect a player to perform a skill if that skill has not been learned through adequate practice. In the sport of volleyball it is critical that the athlete develop his skills through practice to the point that movements become automatic. There is simply not adequate time to evoke the conscious cognitive process; the athlete must rely on reaction. To achieve this automatic level of performance, much practice is necessary with planned progression from simple movements to complex situations.

Volleyball Drills: Volume 1—Individual Training was prepared in response to a need and ever growing demand to facilitate instruction and coaching. The purpose of this publication is to aid coaches and teachers in the selection and planning of volleyball drills essential to effective teaching and practice sessions.

Because of the tremendous involvement of some of our finest United States coaches, an extensive amount of drills has been accumulated. Many of the drills are originals. Most have been gathered and revised over the years as a result of interaction between these contributors and other great teachers, coaches and clinicians from all over the world.

Volleyball Drills: Volume 1—Individual Training is designed as an introductory level to immediately address the needs of our rapidly expanding youth and junior programs in the United States. It is not limited only to this level, however, but can be a valuable tool for the teacher or coach at more advanced levels.

1
PASSING

Chair Passing Drill

Contributor: Amelia Martin
Baptist College at Charleston

Purpose: To work on accuracy and low trajectory in passing; concentration.

Key:

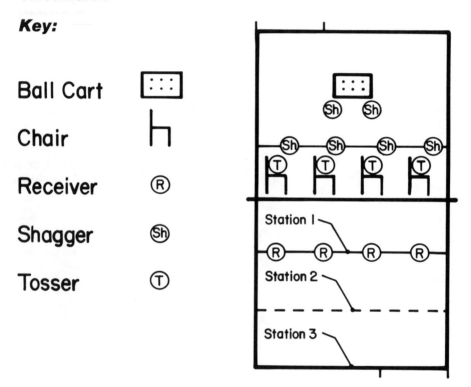

Ball Cart

Chair

Receiver   Ⓡ

Shagger   Ⓢⓗ

Tosser   Ⓣ

Station 1

Station 2

Station 3

Explanation: The players on chairs toss easy balls to the receivers who attempts to pass the ball back into the tossers' hands positioned just above the net. Continue for one minute at Station 1, then back up to Station 2, then to Station 3. Switch receivers and tossers after 3 minutes.

Passing Review Drill

Contributor: Steve Suttich
University of Washington

Purpose: Proper execution of the overhead pass technique.

Key:

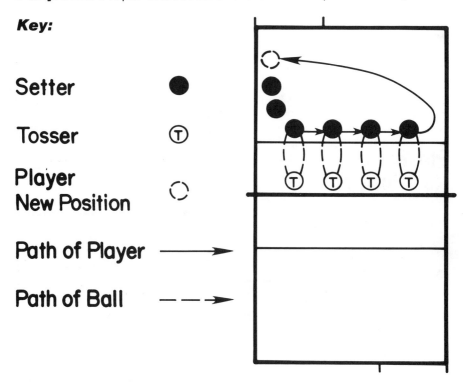

Setter	●
Tosser	Ⓣ
Player New Position	◌
Path of Player	⟶
Path of Ball	– – ⟶

Explanation: The tossers all have a ball. They start the drill by tossing an underhand toss to the player in front of them. The players position their hands, assume proper foot position and set the ball back to the tosser. After setting the ball, they move to their left, stop, and receive another toss until they reach the last tosser, then they return to the end of the line.

Variation:
1. The drill can be done moving from the left to right. Use for both overhand and underhand passing.

Three-Person Line Drill

Contributor: Bob Gambardella
U.S. Military Academy

Purpose: To facilitate proper skill levels, movement and conditioning the players.

Key:

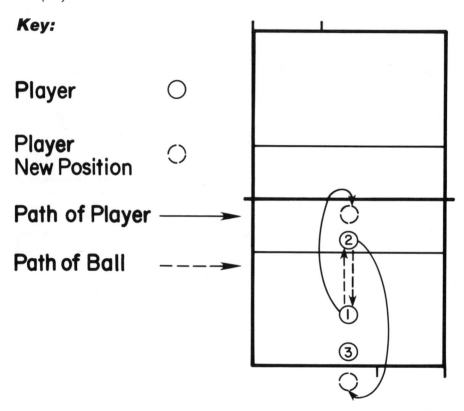

Player   ◯

Player
New Position   ◌

Path of Player ──────▶

Path of Ball   ─ ─ ─ ▶

Explanation: This drill is done in groups of threes. The drill is initiated by player #1 passing the ball to player #2. Player #1 passes the ball and follows the pass to the end of the opposite line. Next, player #2 passes the ball to player #3 and does the same. The drill is continuous and should be done for a specific number of passes.

Variation:
1. This drill can be done using both the overhand and underhand pass.

Cuban Passing WarmUp Drill

Contributor: Ed Halik
U.S. Air Force Academy

Purpose: This exercise is for warmup movement and ball control.

Key:

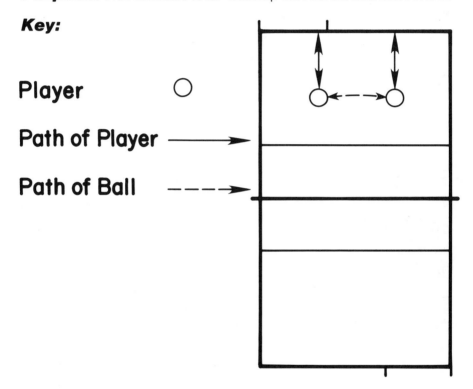

Player   ◯

Path of Player ⟶

Path of Ball ⤏

Explanation: Partners pass a ball back and forth. However, each time players pass they must run to a predetermined spot on the floor, touch the floor and return to the starting point prior to passing the next ball. A specific number of passes or amount of time should be a predetermined goal.

Variations:
1. This drill can be used for overhand or underhand passing.
2. Increases the distance the players must move according to skill level.

Set and Switch Drill

Contributor: Ralph Hippolyte
Nykoping Volleyball Club, Sweden

Purpose: To practice setting and lateral movement; set to a stationary target.

Key:

Coach   Ⓧ

Player   ◯

Shagger   Ⓢⓗ

Ball Cart   ⬚

Path of Player ──────▶

Path of Ball   ── ── ──▶

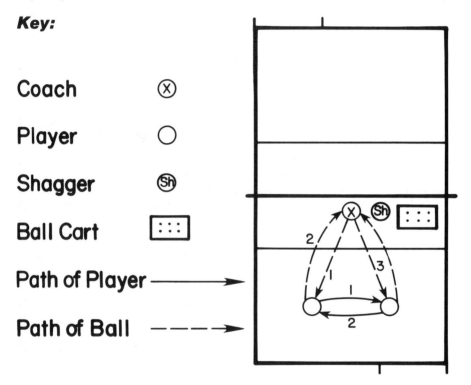

Explanation: The coach tosses to the first player. While the first player is preparing to set back to the coach, the coach quickly tosses to the second player. As soon as a player sets the ball back to the coach, he switches to the other player's position. The drill continues with two balls and both players continually setting and switching.

Variation:
1. Execute the drill using the underhand pass.

Strength Setting Drill

Contributor: Bob Bertucci
University of Tennessee

Purpose: To develop passing control and setting strength.

Key:

Player   ○

Player
New Position   ○

Path of Player   ――――→

Path of Ball   ― ― ― →

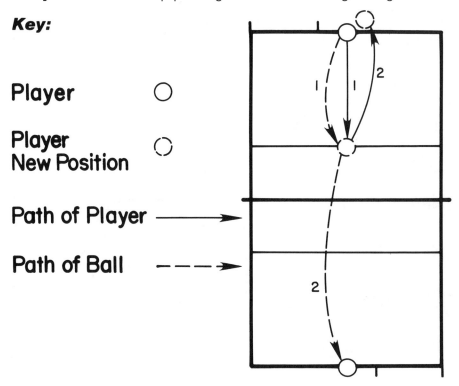

Explanation: Two players start opposite each other on the baselines. The first player with the ball sets it to the closest attack line, runs under the ball, sets it over the net to the second player on the opposite baseline, then returns to the starting position. The second player sets to the closest attack line, runs under the ball, sets it to the first player on the opposite baseline, then returns to starting position. The first player continues the drill by repeating the same sequence.

Bounce Drill

Contributor: Norm Brandl
University of Texas at El Paso

Purpose: To develop the concept of quick recovery from the floor to play another ball, and movement to the ball.

Key:

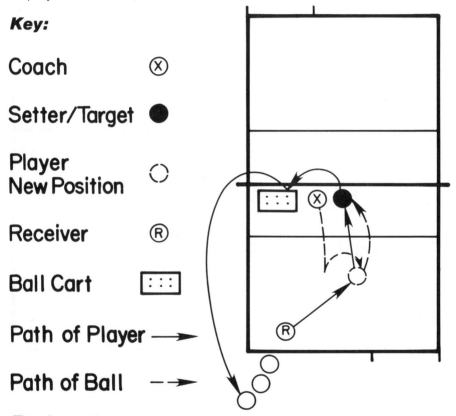

Coach ⊗

Setter/Target ●

Player
New Position ⟲

Receiver Ⓡ

Ball Cart ⬚

Path of Player ⟶

Path of Ball ⇢

Explanation: The first receiver is lying stomach down. The coach bounces the ball on the floor, and the receiver must get up and pass the ball to the target before the ball bounces again. The receiver rotates to become the target, the target shags the ball and places it in the ball cart, then returns to the end of the line.

Variations:
1. How and where the ball is bounced will vary the degree of difficulty.
2. Vary the position of the coach or players.
3. Use the drill for either overhand or underhand passing.

Under the Net Drill

Contributor: Tina Bertucci
University of Tennessee

Purpose: To practice forward and backward movement, accuracy in passing and low movement.

Key:

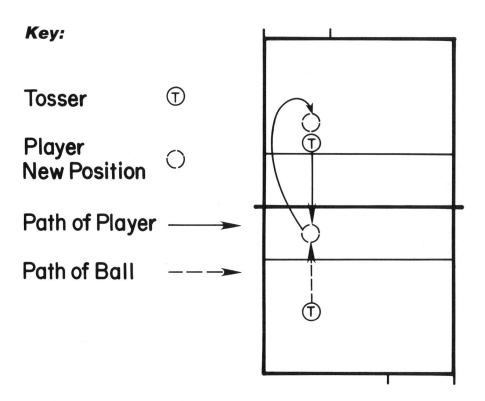

Tosser ⓣ

Player
New Position ◯

Path of Player ⟶

Path of Ball - - ⟶

Explanation: The drill is done in groups of two. The tosser starts the drill by slapping the ball, which signals the player to move towards the tosser in a low comfortable position. As soon as the player breaks the plane of the net, the tosser passes a ball to the player, who underhand passes the ball to the tosser and returns to the original position. The drill can be done continuously for a specified amount of time.

Variations:
1. Use overhand pass instead of underhand pass.
2. The tosser can make the drill continuous by using a self-pass then pass to moving player.

Under and Over the Net Drill

Contributor: Tina Bertucci
University of Tennessee

Purpose: To improve passing and proper movement.

Key:

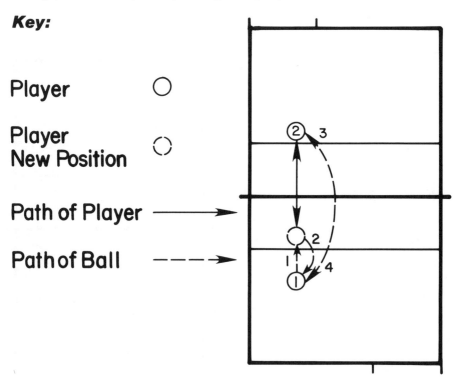

Player ○

Player
New Position ◌

Path of Player ———→

Path of Ball — — —→

Explanation: Player #1 slaps the ball to initiate the drill. Player #2 starts moving towards player #1. Once player #2 passes under the net, player #1 passes the ball to player #2, who in turn passes the ball back to player #1. Then player #2 returns to base position. As player #2 is returning, player #1 passes the ball over the net for player #2 to pass again. The drill repeats itself for a predetermined number of times.

Variation:
1. This drill can be done using both the underhand and overhand pass.

Rumanian Running Drill

Contributor: Taras Liscevych
University of the Pacific

Purpose: To increase passing skill, movement and positioning in passing.

Key:

Player ○

Player
New Position ○

Path of Player ⟶

Path of Ball - - - ➤

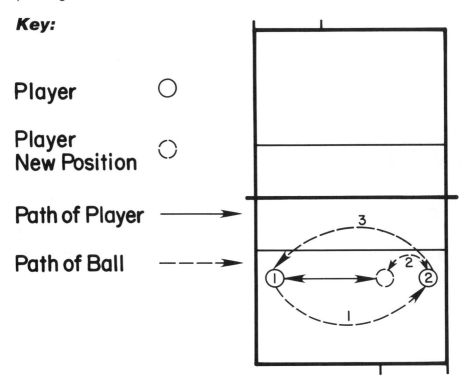

Explanation: Player #1 starts the drill by setting the ball to player #2. Player #1 runs towards player #2 to receive a ball 4-5 feet high directly in front of player #2. Player #1 then sets the ball back to player #2 and backpedals to the starting position.

As player #1 is returning to the starting position, player #2 sets the ball back to the starting position and the drill is repeated.

The drill is continuous until a predetermined number of sets is completed. When player #1 has finished, player #2 will switch and go through the drill.

Rumanian Running Drill: Circle Edition

Contributor: Taras Liscevych
University of the Pacific

Purpose: To increase setting skills along with agility.

Key:

Player   ◯

Player
New Position   ◌

Path of Player   ⎯⎯⎯→

Path of Ball   ⎯ ⎯ ⎯→

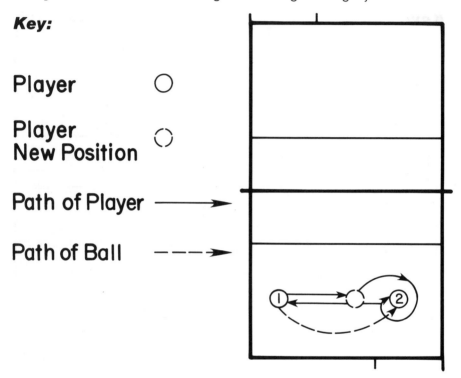

Explanation: Player #1 starts by setting a ball to player #2. After the ball is set player #1 runs towards player #2. Player #2 sets the ball back to player #1, who sets to player #2 and circles around player #2 while player #2 self-sets the ball.

When player #1 finishes the run, player #2 sets the ball back to player #1. Player #1 sets to player #2 and retreats to starting position, where player #2 sets again to continue the drill.

Side to Side Passing Drill

Contributor: Steve Suttich
University of Washington

Purpose: To review underhand passing skill, introduce passing for service reception.

Key:

Player ◯

Receiver Ⓡ

Tosser Ⓣ

Player
New Position ◌

Path of Player ———▶

Path of Ball ---- ▶

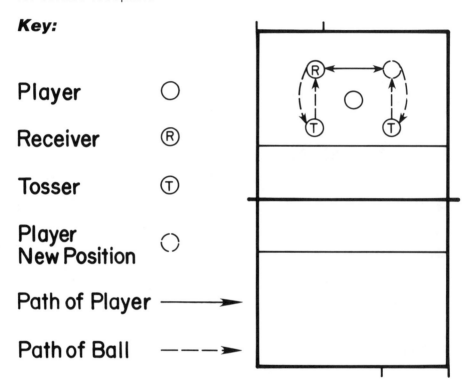

Explanation: Begin the drill with four players — two tossers, one receiver and one player positioned as if in the center front position of a W serve receive formation. Tossers alternate tossing as the receiver switches between the right back (#1) and the left back (#5) positions. Continue the drill for a specific number of passes or a set amount of time.

Variation:
1. Have tossers pass the ball to increase the difficulty of the drill.

Pretzel Drill

Contributor: Bob Gambardella
U.S. Military Academy

Purpose: To promote passing accuracy, proper movement and teamwork.

Key:

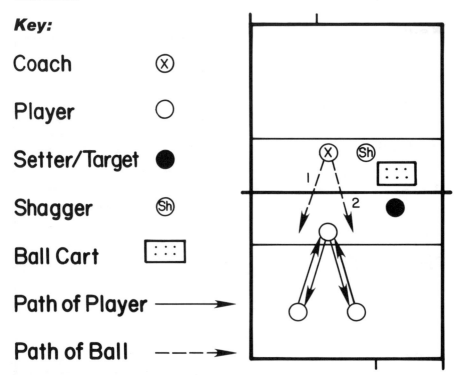

Coach   Ⓧ

Player   ◯

Setter/Target   ●

Shagger   ⓢⓗ

Ball Cart   ⬚

Path of Player   ⟶

Path of Ball   --→

Explanation: The coach starts the drill by tossing a ball to the player in the left back (#5) position, who passes the ball to the target, and immediately switches positons with the player in the center front (#3) position.

Next, the coach tosses a ball to the player in the right back (#1) position. The player passes the ball to the target and immediately the player in position #1 switches with the player in position #3.

The coach then tosses the ball to the #5 position and the drill is repeated once again.

The drill continues until all three players pass five balls in both (#1 and #5) positions.

Kamikaze Line Drill

Contributor: Amelia Martin
Baptist College at Charleston

Purpose: To improve passing accuracy, emergency techniques and communication.

Key:

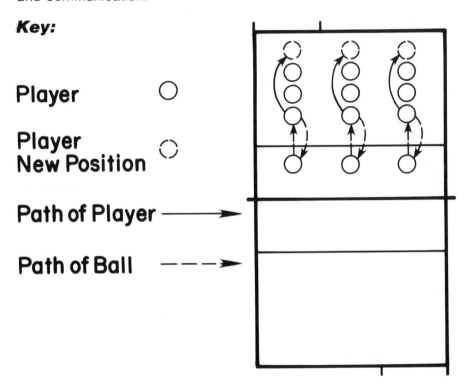

Player   ◯

Player
New Position   ◌

Path of Player ———▶

Path of Ball — — —▶

Explanation: There are three lines with a ball for every line. A lead player for each line faces the line. The lead player tosses a ball toward a player in line, who calls "mine" and passes the ball back to the lead player. After the pass this player returns to the end of the line. Lead players must keep the ball in motion and challenge the next player in line. The ball never stops and a variety of hits should be used by the lead player. The lead player should be switched after a predetermined number of successful passes are made.

Variation:
1. Sufficiently challenge players so they must employ an emergency technique to land after playing the ball.

Up and Back Repeated Setting Drill

Contributor: Ann E. Meyers
University of Dayton

Purpose: To train players to move into a setting position off of a run and increase freeball passing accuracy; an excellent conditioner.

Key:

Coach   Ⓧ

Player   ◯

Player
New Position   ◌

Setter/Target   ●

Shagger   Ⓢⱨ

Ball Cart   ⬚

Path of Player ──▶

Path of Ball   ──▶

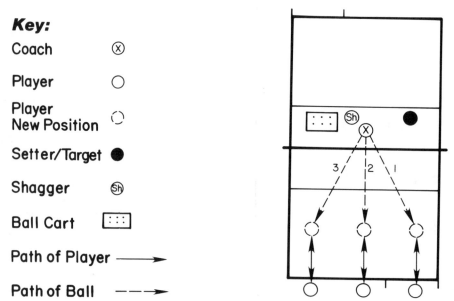

Explanation: The coach starts the drill by tossing the ball about midcourt toward the right back (#1) position. The player in the #1 position is moving forward from the end line. This player must move under the ball and set to the target. As soon as the set is performed the player in middle back (#6) position begins to move in and set the next ball tossed. The third player completes the sequence, moving from the left back (#5) position as soon as the player from #6 sets the ball. When the player from position #5 sets the ball the player from position #1 should have had enough time to backpedal to the baseline and begin the drill again. The drill should continue until each player sets 10 balls to the target.

Variation:

1. The players must backpedal to a wall or a point behind the baseline.

Pass and Go Drill

Contributor: Ralph Hippolyte
Nykoping Volleyball Club, Sweden

Purpose: To teach quick movement, communication and precision.

Key:

Player   ◯

Path of Player ——————▶

Path of Ball   — — — ▶

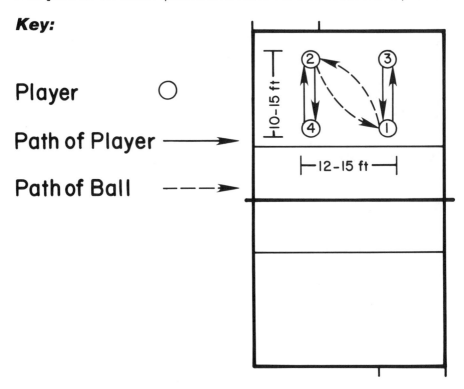

Explanation: Player #1 sets to player #2 and, after setting, player #1 switches places with player #3. Player #2 sets to player #3 (who is now at player #1's original position), then player #2 switches with player #4. Player #3 sets to player #4 and the drill continues.

Variation:
1. This drill can also be done with an underhand pass.

Box Drill

Contributor: Bob Bertucci
University of Tennessee

Purpose: To develop overhand/forearm passing accuracy; communication.

Key:

Player   ◯

Path of Ball ----➤

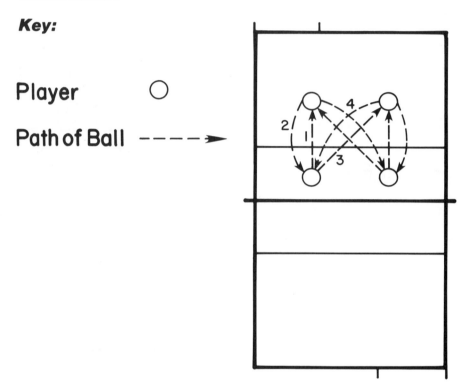

Explanation: Four players set up in a box formation, the two players closest to the net each have a ball. These players simultaneously pass straight across, and the receivers return the ball. Then those closest to the net pass diagonally, and the receivers again return the ball. The same sequence is repeated as the drill continues for a certain number of passes or a time limit.

Lateral Box Drill

Contributor: Tina Bertucci
University of Tennessee

Purpose: To develop lateral movement, footwork and passing accuracy.

Key:

Player   ○

Path of Player ⟶

Path of Ball – – – ⟶

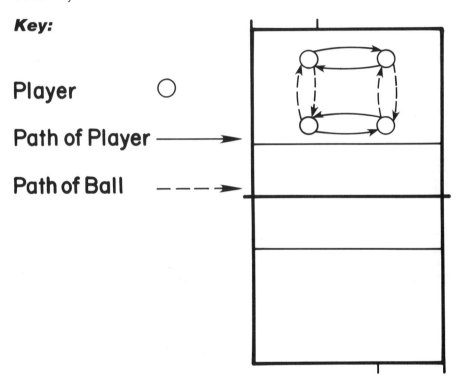

Explanation: Four players set up in a box formation, the two players nearest the net each have a ball. The two players simultaneously pass to the two players furthest from the net, then move laterally and switch positions. The players furthest from the net simply return the pass and also move laterally and switch positions. The drill continues for a specific number of passes.

Variation:
1. This drill can be for underhand and overhand passing.

Clock Bump Drill

Contributor: Arlene Ignico
Austin Peay State University

Purpose: To improve passing accuracy and passing technique.

Key:

Player   ○

Player
New Position   ○

Path of Player ——————➤

Path of Ball — — — ➤

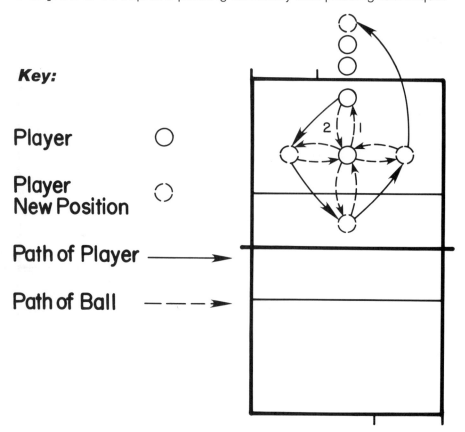

Explanation: One player stands in the center of an imaginary clock. This player passes to the first player in line at the 12 o'clock position. The first player returns the pass and moves to the 9 o'clock, then to the 6 o'clock, then to the 3 o'clock position. After moving around the clock the player goes to the end of the line. The drill continues nonstop until the entire line has gone two times.

Variation:
1. The drill can be done using the overhand pass or digging a spiked ball.

Free Ball Drill

Contributor: Gerald Gregory
University of Wyoming

Purpose: To increase proficiency of left back and right back positions in freeball passing.

Key:

Coach $\otimes$

Player $\bigcirc$

Player
New Position $\bigcirc$

Receiver $\circledR$

Setter/Target   ●

Path of Player   ────▶

Path of Ball   ─ ─ ─▶

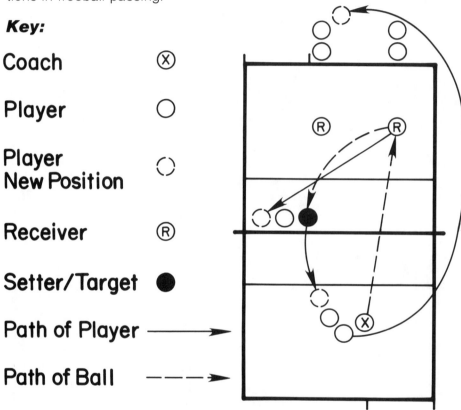

Explanation: The coach throws or hits balls over the net, alternating to either side of the court. The player in the line closest to the ball passes it to the target and goes to the end of the target line. Each target person counts out loud the running total number of perfect passes. The target shags the ball, crosses under the net, hands the ball to the coach and goes to the end of the other line.

Variations:
1. Use the drill allowing only overhand passing.
2. Increase difficulty of freeballs by not hitting near the passing line.

2

SERVING

Wall Serve Drill

Contributor: William T. Odeneal
State University of New York-New Paltz

Purpose: To teach and develop serving skill and technique.

Key:

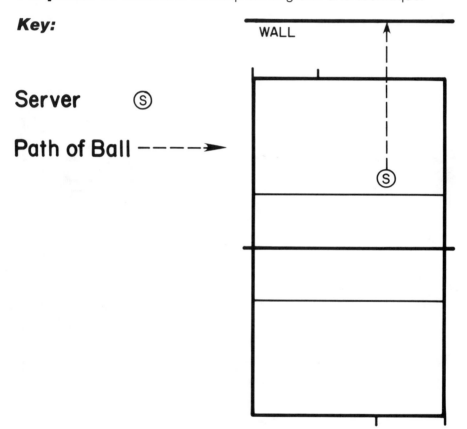

Server   ⓢ

Path of Ball ‒ ‒ ‒ ➤

Explanation: The players practice service above an 8' line marked on a smooth surface wall 30' away from the server. The rebound will come back and player should repeat the drill until the technique is acceptable to the coach.

Variation:
1. Start players close to the wall and gradually move them back.

Mock Serving Drill
Contributor: Bob Bertucci
University of Tennessee

Purpose: To Develop basic mechanics for serving.

Key:

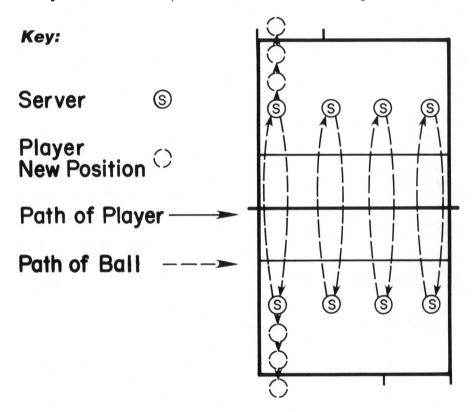

Server   Ⓢ

Player
New Position   ◌

Path of Player ————▶

Path of Ball   — — —▶

Explanation: Two players stand about 15′ feet apart on opposite sides of the net. One starts the drill by executing correct serving technique and serving the ball to the partner. As technique and accuracy improve, the players gradually move toward the base line until accomplishing a full serve.

Line Serve Drill

Contributor: William T. Odeneal
State University of New York-New Paltz

Purpose: To train accuracy and technique in serving.

Key:

Player   ○

Player
New Position   ○

Server   Ⓢ

Shagger   Ⓢⱨ

Path of Player ⟶

Path of Ball ⟶

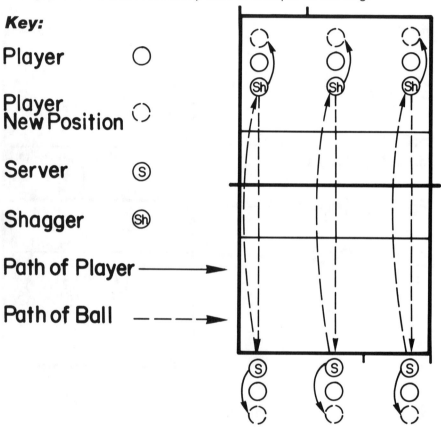

Explanation: Begin with at least six balls. Three lines of players are placed behind the baseline and three other lines are put on the opposite side of the net. The players behind the baseline serve to the players on the opposite side of the net. These players shag the balls and roll them back to the server opposite them. Each player goes to the rear of their line and the next player executes the drill.

Variation:
1. After the serve, the player moves to the end of the opposite line while the shagger retrieves the ball and goes to the end of the serving line.

Full Court Serving Drill

Contributor: Bob Bertucci
University of Tennessee

Purpose: To improve serving technique and accuracy.

Key:

Server ⓢ

Path of Ball ⎯ ⎯ ⎯ ➤

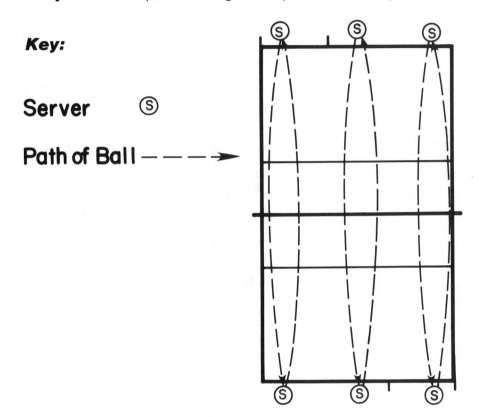

Explanation: Three players start with balls and serve straight ahead to their partners. The partners retrieve the balls and immediately return the serves to the first group of players.

Variations:
1. Tie a rope approximately 2' above the net and have players serve between the net and rope.
2. Have players practice short and long serves.

Serving Consistency Drill

Contributor: Robin Maine
University of Tennessee

Purpose: To simulate game serving pressure.

Key:

Coach   Ⓧ

Server   Ⓢ

Shagger   Ⓢⓗ

Ball Cart   ⌷·:·⌷

Path of Ball   – – – →

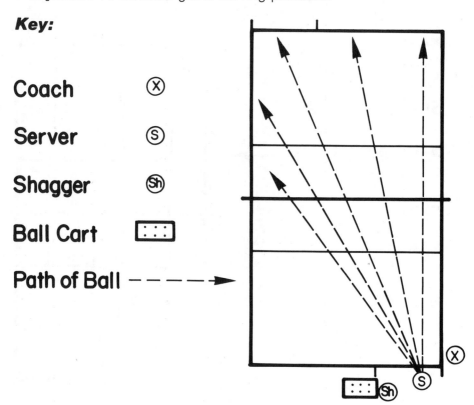

Explanation: One player attempts five serves to predetermined areas. For every miss, the player must serve 10 additional balls.

Variations:
1. For added pressure the coach can stand next to the server.
2. Increase the number or difficulty of the serves.

15-Point Serving Drill

Contributor: Bonnie Kenny
University of Tennessee

Purpose: To create game pressure for the server.

Key:

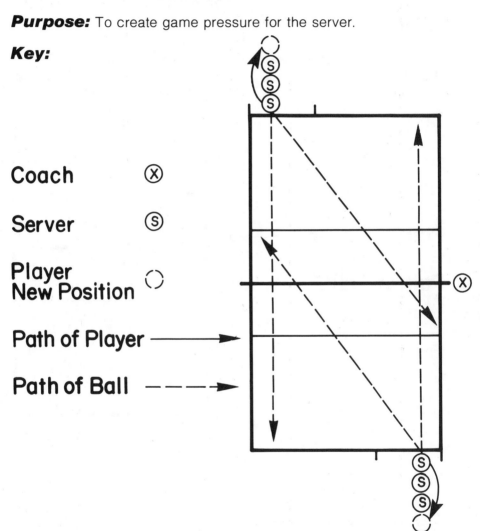

Coach   ⊗

Server   Ⓢ

Player
New Position   ◯

Path of Player ——→

Path of Ball ——→

Explanation: The coach stands at the side of the net. The entire team is divided evenly on the end lines. One player at a time serves, and the coach keeps a running total of how many consecutive serves the team makes. If any player misses a serve, the entire team's total returns to zero. Continue the drill until the team completes a predetermined number or a set amount of time elapses.

Spot Serving Drill

Contributor: Bob Bertucci
University of Tennessee

Purpose: To develop tactical, precise serving.

Key:

Server   Ⓢ

Player
New Position   ◌

Path of Player ——————▶

Path of Ball — — — —▶

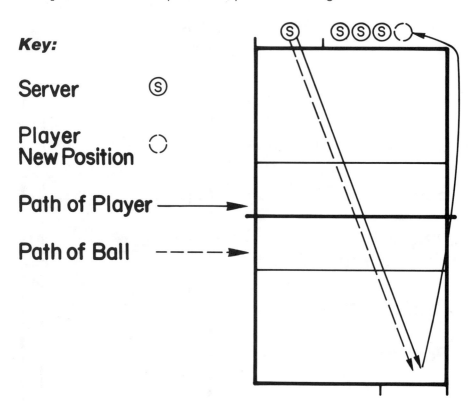

Explanation: The first server serves to the right back (#1) position, retrieves the ball and returns to the end of line. As soon as the first server is out of the way, the next one steps in and serves to position #1. Continue the drill for a set time or a specific number of good serves.

Variation:
1. Practice serving all six court positions.

Nine-Hole Serving Drill

Contributor: Bob Bertucci
University of Tennessee

Purpose: To practice serving accuracy while playing a game.

Key:

Server   Ⓢ

Serving Targets ③ ⑦

Explanation: The court is divided up into nine holes (or areas) designated by numbers placed on the court. The server begins by serving the ball into each area consecutively. A card is kept by each player, recording the number of tries it takes to hit nine holes, or areas. The server must retrieve their own ball each time. The number of tries are added up and the player with the least amount is the winner.

Variation:
1. Set up holes 10 through 18 on the other side of the court and start half the team on the back nine.

Serving Pressure Drill

Contributor: Robin Maine
University of Tennessee

Purpose: To simulate game pressure while serving.

Key:

Coach   (X)

Server   (S)

Player
New Position   ⟲

Path of Player ——————▶

Path of Ball — — — —▶

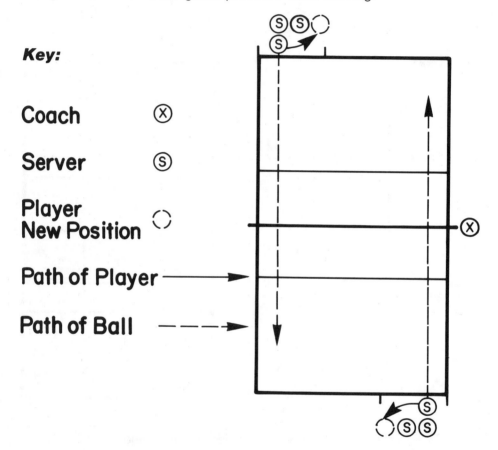

Explanation: Players are divided into two equal teams. Each player takes a turn serving while all the others are watching. One point is awarded for a successful serve and two points are taken away for a missed serve. The first team to reach 15 is the winner.

Variation:
1. Serve to a predetermined area.

Accu-Speed Serving Drill

Contributor: Bonnie Kenny
University of Tennessee

Purpose: A pressure drill for serving. Accuracy and repetition of correct serving mechanics are its focus.

Key:

Coach   Ⓧ

Server   Ⓢ

Shagger   Ⓢⓗ

Ball Cart   ⌷

Path of Ball   – – – →

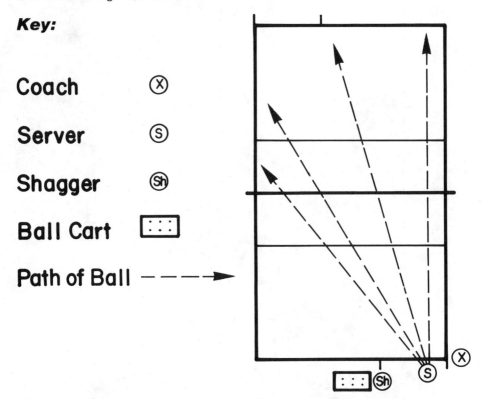

Explanation: The coach sets a one- to two-minute time limit. One player stands on the end line in the serving position. Other players are shagging balls so the server has a constant supply. The coach stands near the server, timing and counting how many consecutive serves the player achieves in the given amount of time. Once the server misses, a new player replaces him.

Variations:
1. Require a server to serve to a specific area.
2. Award point values: 3 points for a tough serve to the correct area; 2 points for a legal serve to the correct area; 1 point for a legal serve.

3

SERVICE RECEPTION

Players vs Coach Drill

Contributor: Bob Bertucci
University of Tennessee

Purpose: Service reception accuracy.

Key:

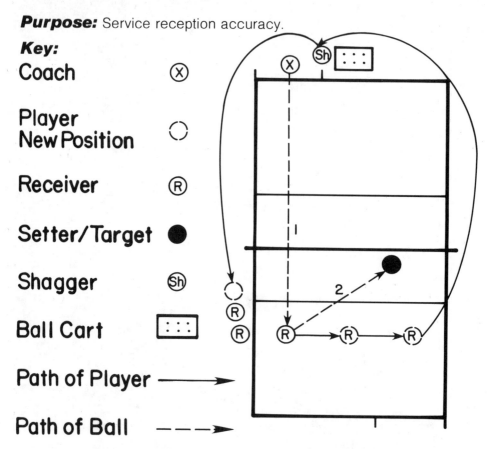

Coach	Ⓧ
Player New Position	◌
Receiver	Ⓡ
Setter/Target	●
Shagger	Ⓢⓗ
Ball Cart	⬚
Path of Player	⟶
Path of Ball	– – ⟶

Explanation: The coach starts the drill by serving down the line. The coach should serve to any area of the last one-third of the court. The player starting the drill tries to receive service and pass it directly to the target. After each pass the receiver moves one position to the right. For each pass the players precisely deliver to the target, they receive one point. The first to reach 15 points wins the game.

Variations:
1. Run receiving line from right to left side.
2. Start receiving line at the net to train backward movement or at the baseline to develop forward movement patterns.

5-Position Serve Receive Drill

Contributor: Russ Rose
Penn State University

Purpose: To enhance the players' ability to receive serves in all areas of the court.

Key:

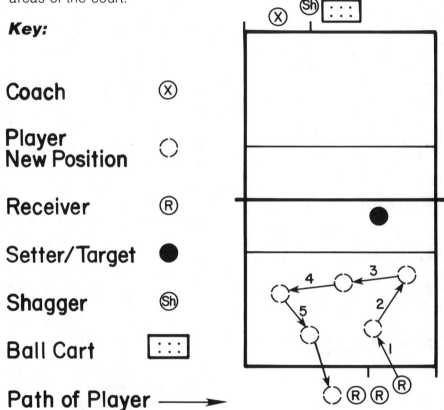

Coach	Ⓧ
Player New Position	◌
Receiver	Ⓡ
Setter/Target	●
Shagger	Ⓢⱨ
Ball Cart	⟦∶∶∶⟧
Path of Player	——→

Explanation: The coach serves to each of the five positions of the W serve reception pattern. Each player passes five balls in succession at all positions and then returns to the end of the line. The drill is continued until each has gone through the circuit three times.

Variation:

1. The setter sets the ball to one of two hitters positioned at left and right front (#4, #2) positions. They can hit various shots, dinks or roll shots to designated area.

Go for Two Receiving Drill

Contributor: Bob Bertucci
University of Tennessee

Purpose: To improve serve reception in the two deep positions of a W formation.

Key:

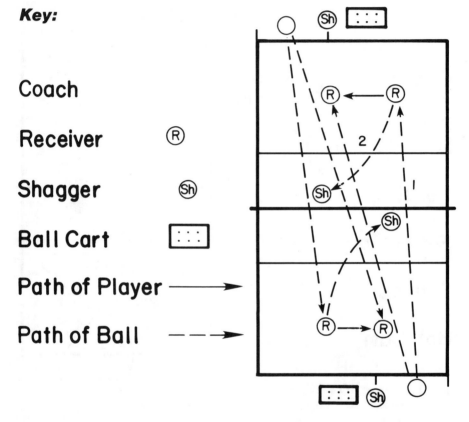

Coach

Receiver   Ⓡ

Shagger   Ⓢⓗ

Ball Cart   ⦙⋯⦙

Path of Player   ⟶

Path of Ball   --⟶

Explanation: The coach alternates serving the left back (#5) position and the right back (#1) position of a W serve receive formation. The receiver must pass the ball to the target, switch, and immediately pass again. The same player continues until two passes are made directly to the target consecutively.

Variations:
1. Move from right to left.
2. Do not serve directly to the player. This increases the difficulty of the pass.

Run and Spin Drill

Contributor: Ralph Hippolyte
Nykoping Volleyball Club, Sweden

Purpose: To develop speed and spatial orientation in receiving serves.

Key:

Coach	Ⓧ
Player New Position	◌
Receiver	Ⓡ
Setter/Target	●
Shagger	Ⓢⓗ
Ball Cart	⬚
Path of Player	⟶
Path of Ball	⤍

Explanation: When the coach slaps the ball, the first receiver sprints to the left back (#5) position on the other side of the net. As soon as the receiver reaches the net, the coach serves to the left back area of the court. The receiver passes to the target and returns to the end of the line.

Variations:
1. The coach serves to different positions on the court.
2. The coach varies the type of serve.

Reaction Receiving Drill

Contributor: Ralph Hippolyte
Nykoping Volleyball Club, Sweden

Purpose: To train quick movement in service reception.

Key:

Coach on Table

Player

Player
New Position

Receiver

Setter/Target

Shagger

Ball Cart

Path of Player

Path of Ball

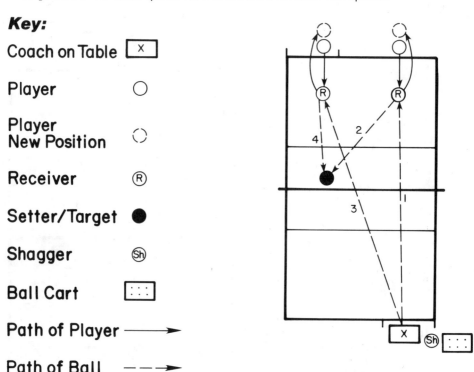

Explanation: The coach stands on a table and serves to a receiver in the left back (#5) position. This player passes to a target and returns to the end of the line. The coach then serves to another receiver in the right back (#1) position. A new receiver switches places as soon as the receiver passes a ball. This drill should be continued until time expires or a specific number of successful passes are completed.

Variations:

1. Position the receivers in other areas similar to your receiving pattern.
2. Adjust the distance of the table from the baseline, from which the coach is serving.

Two-Man Serve Reception Drill

Contributor: Darlene Bailey
Boise State

Purpose: To improve serve reception, teamwork and communication.

Key:

Coach ⊗

Receiver Ⓡ

Shagger Ⓢⓗ

Ball Cart ⬚⋯

Path of Ball — — — →

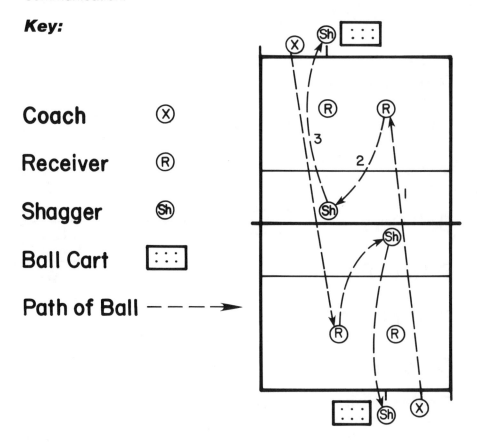

Explanation: The coach alternates serving all areas of the court, as tough as possible. Receivers must pass every ball and communicate short, in, out, mine, etc. After a designated time or a certain number of serves, receivers switch positions and pass again.

Accuracy Passing Drill

Contributor: Eugenia Kriebel
Butler University

Purpose: To improve accuracy in passing.

Key:

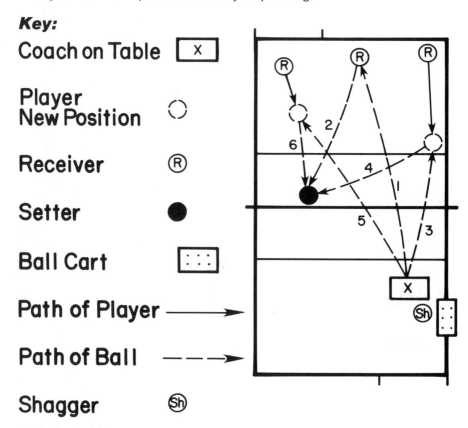

Coach on Table

Player
New Position

Receiver

Setter

Ball Cart

Path of Player

Path of Ball

Shagger

Explanation: Three receivers start on the baseline. The coach is on a table located on the opposite side of the net. The coach serves, hits or tosses balls to the receivers in all directions, depending on skill level and weaknesses. The setter acts as a target and catches the passes. If the setter keeps a pivot foot in place the receiver earns a point. Each receiver must earn 15 points before moving to the next position.

Variations:
1. Work in teams of three and rotate when the team gets 15 points.
2. Start receivers at the attack line.

Triangle Serve Receive Drill

Contributor: Chris S. Wyman
Northeastern University

Purpose: To improve passing accuracy and communication in service reception.

Key:

Server   Ⓢ

Receiver   Ⓡ

Setter/Target   ●

Path of Ball   — — —➤

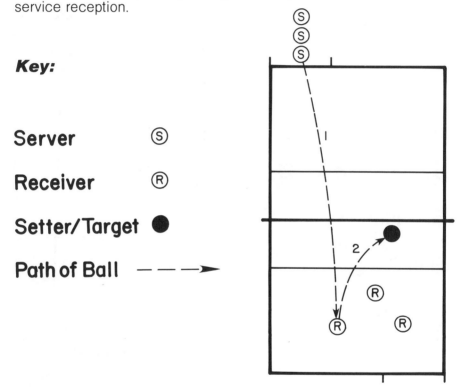

Explanation: Each server alternately serves 15 balls, aiming for the center front or the right or left back receiving positions. Receivers attempt to pass to the target, rotating after every three serves. The serving group counts the number of good serves, and the receivers count the number of good passes. The group with the highest total of good serves and good passes wins.

Variations:
1. Move receivers to the left front, center front and left back positions.
2. Move receivers to the right front, center front and right back positions.
3. Have the target set every pass.

One-Third Serve Receive Drill

Contributor: Bob Bertucci
University of Tennessee

Purpose: To develop team service reception for one-third of a W formation.

Key:

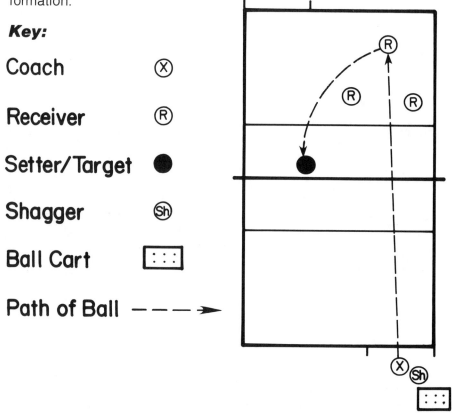

Coach   ⓧ

Receiver   Ⓡ

Setter/Target   ●

Shagger   Ⓢⱨ

Ball Cart   [:::]

Path of Ball   — — — ➤

Explanation: The coach serves down the line to the left third of the court. Three players are positioned at left side of a W service reception formation. They are responsible for communicating and passing the ball to the target. The players should rotate after a specific number of balls are passed to the target.

Variations:
1. Run the same drill to the center and right third of the W formation.
2. Vary the distance the coach stands from the net based on the skill level.

Service Reception Drill

Contributor: Jodi Manore
University of Toledo

Purpose: To improve service reception and serving.

Key:

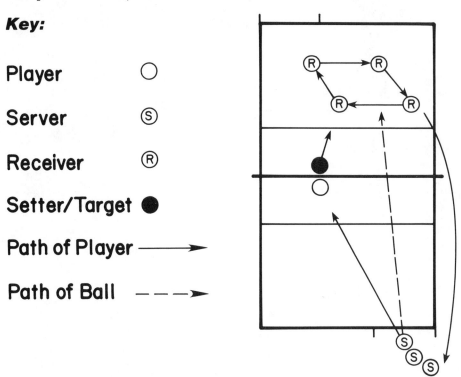

Player	○
Server	Ⓢ
Receiver	Ⓡ
Setter/Target	●
Path of Player	—————▶
Path of Ball	— — —▶

Explanation: Four or five receivers are used, based on a team's actual serve receive formation. Two players are at the net and the rest are serving. The server serves and, if the ball is passed to the target, the receivers rotate. If not, the receiver committing the error goes to the serving line and is replaced by the target. The server takes the vacant position at the net. Serving is continuous; players must rotate or switch quickly. Continue the drill for a particular number of good passes or a limited amount of time.

Variations:
1. Have a group of receivers stay on one side for a particular number of serves and keep track of passing accuracy. Allow missed serves to count as a good play for the receivers.
2. Vary the type of receiving formation.

4

SETTING

Half-Circle Setting Drill

Contributor: Steve Suttich
University of Washington

Purpose: To teach proper setting technique.

Key:

Coach   Ⓧ

Setter   ●

Shagger   ⓈⒽ

Player
New Position   ◌

Ball Cart   ⬚

Path of Player   ⟶

Path of Ball   ⤏

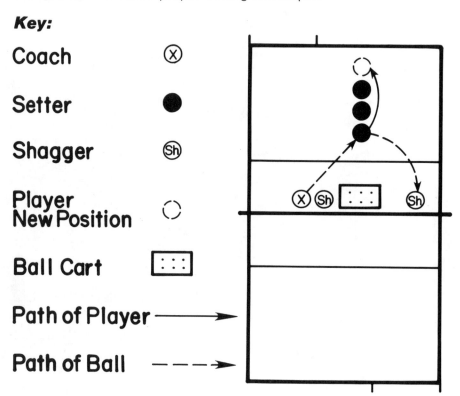

Explanation: The coach tosses a ball directly above the head of the first player in line, who overhand passes to the shagger in the left front (#4) position. The player then moves to the end of the line. Continue the drill until the coach feels the players are executing the skill correctly.

Variations:
1. Set to the right front (#2) position.
2. Bounce the ball, forcing the player to learn how to move under the ball before setting.

Backcourt Setting Drill

Contributor: Ralph Hippolyte
Nykoping Volleyball Club, Sweden

Purpose: To teach backcourt setting.

Key:

Coach	⊗
Player	○
Player New Position	◌
Setter/Target	●
Shagger	Ⓢⓗ
Ball Cart	⊡
Path of Player	——→
Path of Ball	– – –→

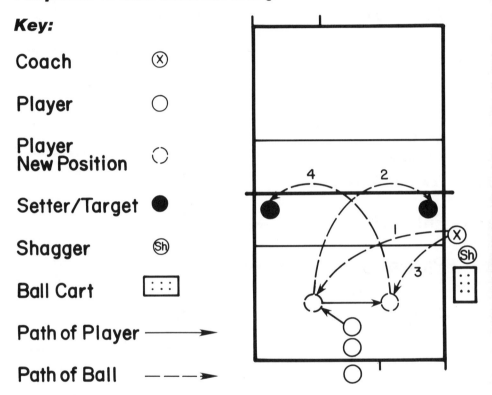

Explanation: The coach tosses a deep ball to the left back (#5) position. The first player runs, gets in position behind the ball and sets a high ball to the right front (#2) position. The coach then tosses a deep ball to the right back (#1) position, and the same player moves quickly into position behind the ball to set a high ball to the left front (#4) position. This player returns to the end of the line and the next player begins. Continue for a certain number of repetitions or until time has expired.

Variation:
1. The coach tosses from different positions and from the other side of the net.

Continuous Backcourt Setting Drill

Contributor: Bob Bertucci
University of Tennessee

Purpose: To develop backcourt setting and the ability to set along the net.

Key:

Player   ◯

Player
New Position   ◌

Path of Player ⟶

Path of Ball ⟶

Explanation: The first backcourt player begins by setting the ball to the left front (#4) position. The left front player sets the ball to the right front (#2) position. The right front player sets to either the right back (#1) position or the center back (#6) position. The next backcourt player in line continues the drill by moving to the ball and setting to the #4 position. Continue the drill for a particular number of sets or a specific time limit.

Variations:
1. Have the backcourt players set from positions #5 or #6 to position #2.
2. Have the first setter at the net approach the jumpset.

The Great Chase Drill

Contributor: Ann E. Meyers
University of Dayton

Purpose: To practice running down a ball going out of play, teamwork and communication.

Key:

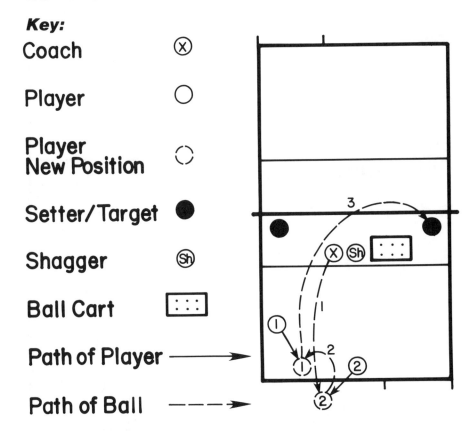

Coach   ⊗

Player   ○

Player
New Position   ◌

Setter/Target   ●

Shagger   ⑤ʰ

Ball Cart   ⌶⋮⌶

Path of Player   ⟶

Path of Ball   ⟶

Explanation: The coach slaps the ball and tosses a high ball outside the court. On the slap, two defensive players turn and sprint toward the ball. The player closest to the ball calls "mine" and passes the ball to the other player who is following. The second player then sets to either target and the drill continues until a specific goal is reached.

Variations:
1. Work the drill from the right and center back defense positions.
2. Have the targets spike the ball.

Haitian Backsetting Drill

Contributor: Ralph Hippolyte
Nykoping Volleyball Club, Sweden

Purpose: To practice backsetting, and to develop audible cues in directional setting.

Key:

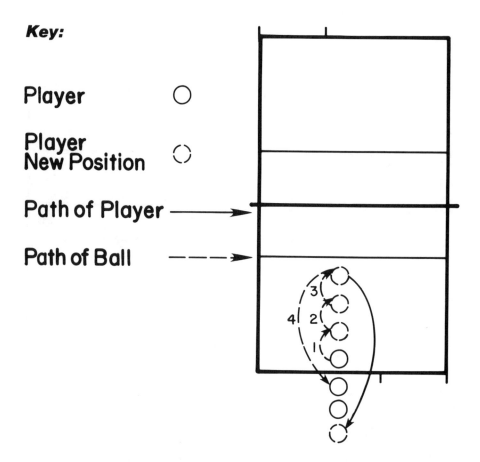

Player   ◯

Player
New Position   ◌

Path of Player ——→

Path of Ball   ---→

Explanation: The drill begins with three players in each group. The first player sets the ball three times to himself while walking forward. After the third set the next player in line (positioned at the end line) calls the player's name so that the player setting can backset to that target. After this player executes the backset, he runs to the end of the line. The drill can be done until each player has backset five times.

Turn and Set Drill

Contributor: Ralph Hippolyte
Nykoping Volleyball Club, Sweden

Purpose: To teach the setter how to change direction and deliver an accurate set; to develop a fake technique in setting.

Key:

Player   ◯

Setter   ●

Path of Player   ⟶

Path of Ball   ⇢

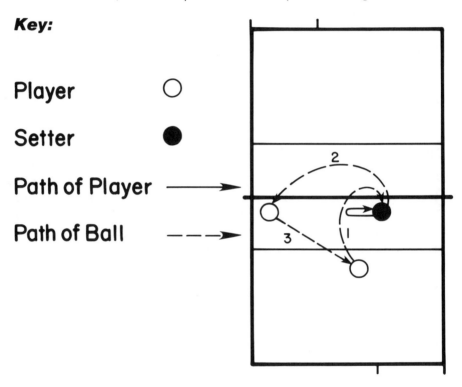

Explanation: The backcourt player starts the drill by setting the ball in front of the setter. The setter steps forward and pivots as if to set the right front (#2) position, but instead backsets to the player in the left front (#4) position. This player passes to the backcourt player, and the drill begins again.

Sprint and Set Drill

Contributor: Ralph Hippolyte
Nykoping Volleyball Club, Sweden

Purpose: To increase the setter's range and speed.

Key:

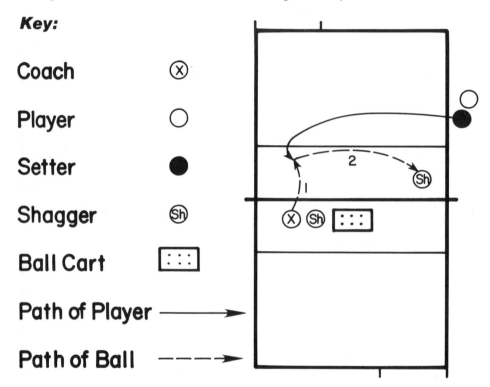

Coach	⊗
Player	○
Setter	●
Shagger	(Sh)
Ball Cart	⬚
Path of Player	——→
Path of Ball	– – →

Explanation: Before tossing a high ball over the net to the attack line, the coach slaps the ball to signal the first setter to begin sprinting. This player comes behind and under the ball, sets a high ball 3' from the net and 3' from the sideline to a stationary target in the left front (#4) position.

Variations:
1. Replace the shagger with a spiker, working two skills in the same drill.
2. Work the drill with the setter passing the ball to the right front (#2) position.
3. Switch sides and work the drill, setting to #2

Move Setter Drill

Contributor: Darlene A. Kluka
Texas Woman's University

Purpose: To develop movement, accuracy, consistency, and endurance for setters in a multiple offense system.

Key:

Coach	⊗
Player	○
Setter	●
Shagger	ⓢ
Chair	⌐
Ball Cart	⬚
Path of Player	—→
Path of Ball	− − →

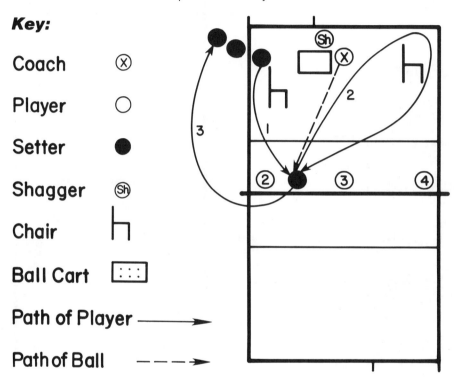

Explanation: The coach tosses between the players in position #2 and #3. The setter starts in the #1 position and runs around a chair to the target area. The setter sets to the players in the #1 position and runs around a chair to the target area. The setter sets to the players in either the #4, #3 or #2 positions. The setter then runs around a chair at the #5 position. The coach tosses another ball and the setter must set it to one of the hitting positions.

Variations:
1. Set to a variety of positions.
2. Vary heights, according to your team's offensive system.
3. Add blockers, then diggers.

Down and Up Drill

Contributor: Bob Bertucci
University of Tennessee

Purpose: To develop setting accuracy after movement.

Key:

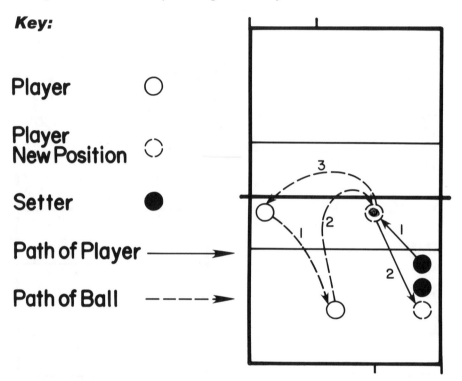

Player   ◯

Player New Position   ◌

Setter   ●

Path of Player   ——▶

Path of Ball   - - - -▶

Explanation: The player in the left front (#4) position starts the drill by setting to the backcourt player. At the same time the first setter, who is lying on the floor, gets up and runs to the setting position. The backcourt player passes the ball to the target area, and the setter must execute an accurate set to the #4 position. As soon as the player at #4 touches the ball, the second setter gets up and runs to the net.

Variations:
1. Have the setters practice different sets.
2. Have setters penetrate from different positions.

Setting Weave Drill

Contributor: Jackie Bartlett
University of North Carolina-Wilmington

Purpose: To practice setting after moving; develop setting accuracy.

Key:

Coach   Ⓧ

Player   ○

Player
New Position   ◌

Shagger   Ⓢⓗ

Ball Cart   ⬚

Path of Player ——▶

Path of Ball   ----▶

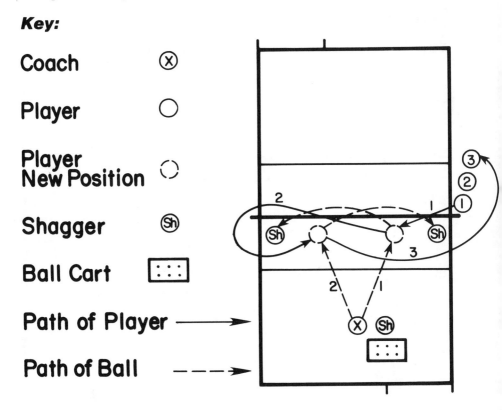

Explanation: Three players form a single-file line on the sideline near the net. The coach stands on the opposite side of the net in the middle of the court. Two shaggers, one on each sideline, are positioned on the same side as the coach. The coach tosses and player #1 comes under the net and sets to the shagger on the far sideline. Player #1 then goes back under the net and around the pole on the far side of the court. Player #1 then sets to the other shagger and runs around the pole to the end of the line. Players #2 and #3 repeat the same movements. The drill continues until each shagger receives 25 good sets.

Four-Corner Bread and Butter Drill

Contributor: Cheryl Alexander
California State College-Bakersfield

Purpose: To practice setting, especially from backcourt.

Key:

Player   ○

Path of Ball — — — ➤

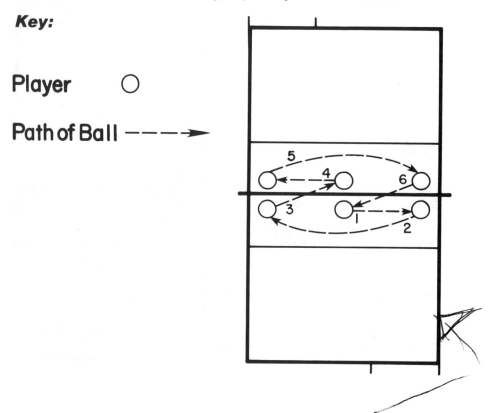

Explanation: The drill begins in the server's corner. Player #1 sets the ball along the baseline to the left back (#5) position. This player sets diagonally to the right front (#2) position. The player here sets along the net to the left front (#4) position. This player sets diagonally back to the server's corner, and the sequence begins again. Players rotate by following their sets.

Variation:

1. Two balls can be used. The second ball should be started after the first ball is set diagonally to the #2 position.

Continuous Setting Drill

Contributor: Bob Bertucci
University of Tennessee

Purpose: To improve setting to different positions on the net.

Key:

Player ○

Path of Ball – – – – ➤

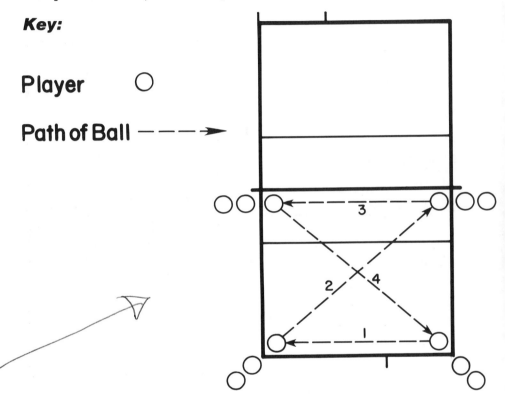

Explanation: The player in the center front (#3) position on either side of the net may start the drill by setting it to the right front (#2) position on the same side then continues the drill by setting to the player in #2 position. The player in #2 position then sets the ball to the player in the left front (#4) position. The player in #4 position then sets over the net to the player in the #3 position. The player in #3 position on the same side, who in turn sets to the player in #3 position and the drill cycle begins again. This drill should be done for 5 complete cycles without an error.

Variation:
1. Start two players in each position with one switching after each set.

Setting Suicide Drill

Contributor: Lucy E. Ticki
Seton Hall University

Purpose: To develop control of overhead passing and build quick movement patterns.

Key:

Player   ◯

Player
New Position   ◌

Path of Player   ──────→

Path of Ball   ─ ─ ─ →

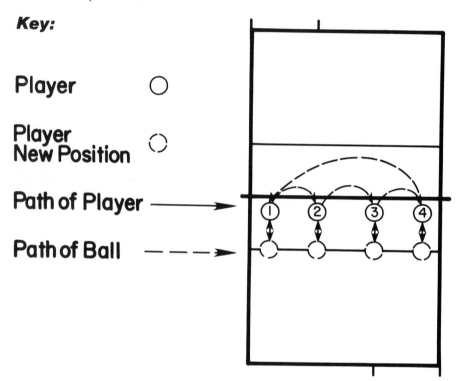

Explanation: Four players line up along the net. Player #1 begins with a set to self, then sets to player #2. Player #2 in turn self-sets, turns under the ball and sets it to player #3. Player #3 does the same as player #2, but sets to player #4. Player #4 then sets the length of the net back to player #1. After each player sets, they must touch the attack line and return in time to pass the next ball. Continue for 1 minute then switch players.

Variations:
1. Make athletes touch the baseline.
2. Execute an emergency technique to the attack line.

Continuous Jump Setting Drill

Contributor: Ralph Hippolyte
Nykoping Volleyball Club, Sweden

Purpose: To teach setting, setting to a spot, and communication.

Key:

Player   O

Path of Player   ⟶

Path of Ball   ⟶

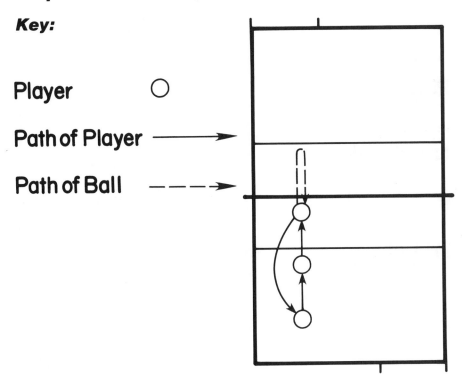

Explanation: The first player jumpsets straight up, then sprints approximately 20′ from the net. The second player runs to the net, jumpsets and sprints the same distance. The third player repeats the same sequence. The height of each set is determined by the progress being made by the next setter. Continue for a specific number of repetitions or until time expires.

Variations:
1. Have players use regular sets.
2. Set up several stations of the drill.
3. Have players sprint to the baseline between sets.

Jumpsetter Drill

Contributor: Ralph Hippolyte
Nykoping Volleyball Club, Sweden

Purpose: To teach jumpsetting to spikers.

Key:

Player ○

Player
New Position ○

Path of Player ——→

Path of Ball – – –→

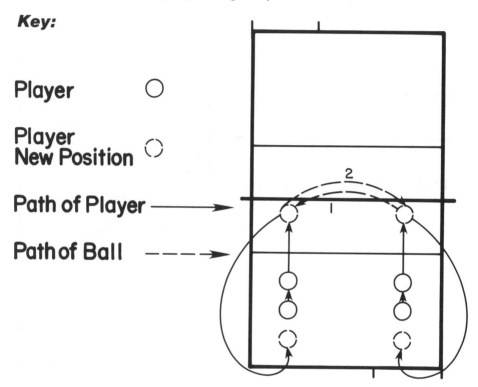

Explanation: The player in the right front (#2) position starts the drill by setting to the left front (#4) position. The first in that line approaches, jumps and sets back to #2 position. The next player approaches to #2 position and jumpsets back to #4 position, repeating the drill. After jumpsetting, players sprint back to touch the baseline, then move to the end of their lines. The drill continues for 20 consecutive jumpsets or a specific amount of time.

5

SPIKING

Hitting Approach Progression Drill

Contributor: Steve Suttich
University of Washington

Purpose: To teach and develop the correct approach steps for spiking.

Key:

Hitter

Path of Player

Foot Position

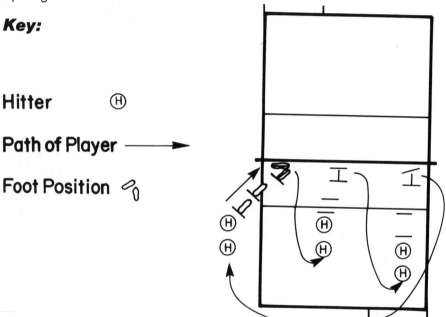

Explanation: The drill begins by the coach placing tape in specific positions appropriately spaced as shown in the diagram. The spacing is based on the stride length of the athletes performing the drill. The position of the tape is identical to the actual steps taken for the approach. Each step of the approach increases in length and speed. The hitters start in a single line and approach the net with each step of their approach landing on a piece of tape. After the approach and jump, upon landing, the hitter immediately moves to the end of the next line. Repeat this sequence a set number of times.

Variations:
1. Break down the full approach into three segments. Drill the step/ close segment, adding first the second and third segments later.
2. Have a coach or player stand on a chair and have the hitter spike a held ball.

Spike-It Drill

Contributor: Lynn Fielitz
University of Tennessee

Purpose: To teach proper spike approach, arm extension and ball contact.

Key:

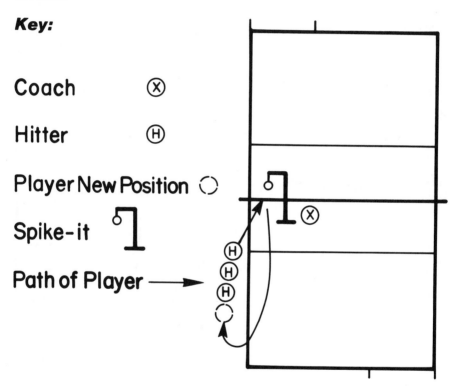

Coach   ⊗

Hitter   Ⓗ

Player New Position   ◯

Spike-it

Path of Player ⟶

Explanation: A Spike-It—a portable device which suspends a volleyball above the net—is placed in the left front (#4) position. A group of three hitters are in a single-file line approximately 10' from the net. The drill begins with the first hitter in line making a correct approach, jump and swing, contacting the suspended ball. The hitter then returns to the back of the line and the second hitter performs the skill. The drill can be repeated for a set number of hits or length of time.

Variation:

1. The coach, standing on a chair, holds a ball above the net for the hitter to spike.

Stationary Partner Spiking Drill

Contributor: Lynn Fielitz
University of Tennessee

Purpose: To learn proper body position and the up-and-over arm swing for spiking.

Key:

Hitter   (H)

Path of Ball — — — ➤

Foot Position

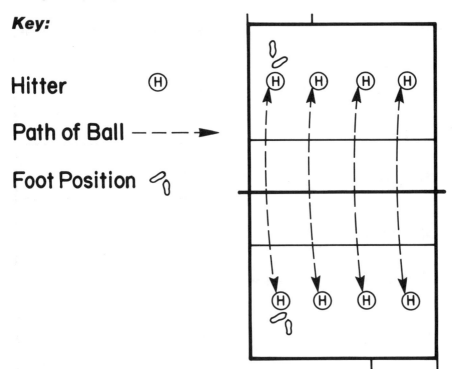

Explanation: The hitters are divided into groups of two. They are positioned in the middle of each court approximately 15' from the net. The hitter assumes the proper foot position, tosses the ball overhead and executes an up-and-over arm swing, hitting the ball over the net to a partner. The partner shags the ball, assumes the proper foot position and repeats the drill. Continue for a set number of hits or length of time.

Variation:
1. The hitter tosses the ball directly in front of the hitting shoulder, jumps and spikes the ball.

Endurance Hitting Drill

Contributor: Jackie Bartlett
University of North Carolina-Wilmington

Purpose: To develop hitting endurance and timing.

Key:

Coach   ⊗

Hitter   Ⓗ

Player
New Position ◌

Shagger   Ⓢⓗ

Chair   ⌐

Ball Cart   ⸤∷∷⸥

Path of Player ──▶

Path of Ball ── ─▶

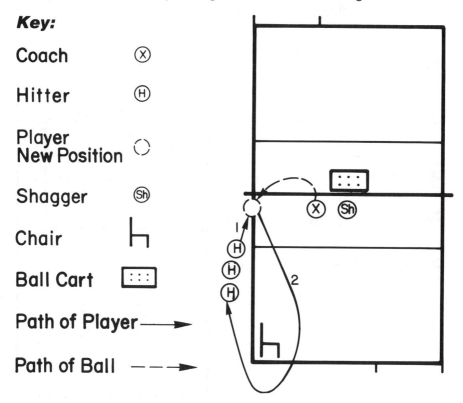

Explanation: Three players form a single line at the 10' line. The coach tosses a ball and the first hitter approaches and spikes, then runs around a chair placed on the endline. As soon as the first hitter is out of the way, the coach tosses and the second hitter repeats the same sequence. The drill continues until the group gets 20 good hits.

Variations:
1. The hitters must spike to a certain position on the court in order to be counted as a good it.
2. Vary the types of tosses and positions from which the toss is executed.
3. Add blockers.

Bounce and Spike Drill

Contributor: Bob Schneck
University of Rhode Island

Purpose: To teach players to correctly position their bodies to the ball and to execute the proper approach step.

Key:

Hitter Ⓗ

Shagger ⓈⒽ

Path of Player ———▶

Path of Ball ––––▶

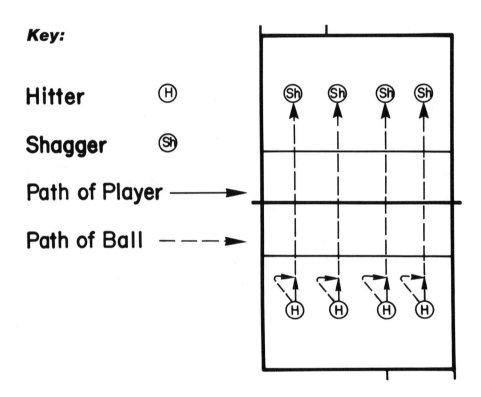

Explanation: The hitters forcefully bounce the balls to the floor in front of their bodies so that the balls rebound above their heads. They then adjust to the ball and use the proper approach steps to spike the balls across the net to their respective shaggers.

Variations:
1. Vary the direction of the bounce.
2. Require the spikers to hit a specific area on the court.

Scatter Spiking Drill

Contributor: Bob Gambardella
U.S. Military Academy

Purpose: To train spike approach and correct body positioning while spiking a ball.

Key:

Coach	⊗
Hitter	Ⓗ
Player New Position	◯
Shagger	ⓢⱨ
Ball Cart	⊡
Path of Player	⟶
Path of Ball	⤙⟶

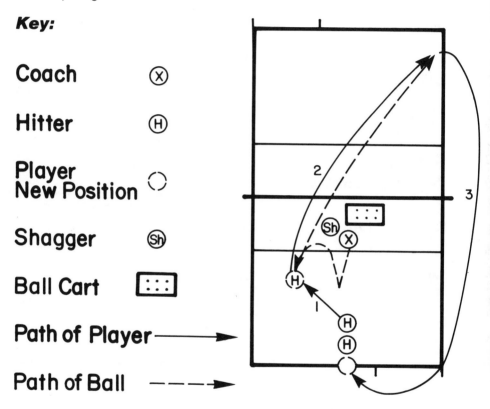

Explanation: The drill is initiated by the shagger handing a ball to the coach. The hitters line up single file (middle deep) on the court. The coach bounces the ball and the first hitter approaches, positioning himself correctly to spike the ball. This drill runs for a predetermined time or set amount of successful spikes.

Variations:
1. Bounce balls to opposite side shown in diagram.
2. Require hitters to spike balls to a specific area of the court.

Japanese Tossing Drill

Contributor: Robin Maine
University of Tennessee

Purpose: To train approach and arm swing for the quick middle hit.

Key:

Coach   ⊗

Hitter   Ⓗ

Player
New Position   ◯

Path of Player   ——————▶

Path of Ball   – – – ▶

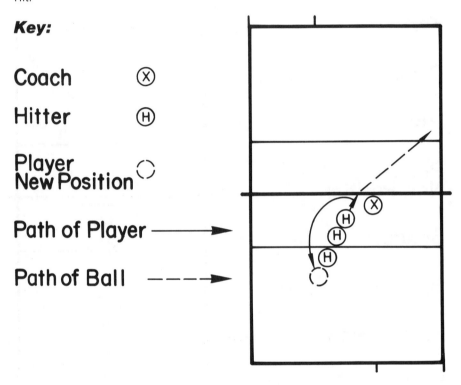

Explanation: Each player approaches the net, executing the proper approach steps and arm swing. The coach tosses the ball directly into the spiker's hand as the spiker is swinging.

Variations:
1. Vary the coach's tossing position.
2. Toss the ball for a spiker attacking for a half-shoot.

Variable Spiking Drill

Contributor: Mario Treibitch
Puerto Rican Women's National Team

Purpose: To train players to spike balls being tossed from different positions and varying speeds and trajectories.

Key:

Coach   Ⓧ

Hitter   Ⓗ

Player
New Position   ◯

Shagger   Ⓢⓗ

Ball Cart   ⬚

Path of Player ⟶

Path of Ball   ‒ ‒ ➤

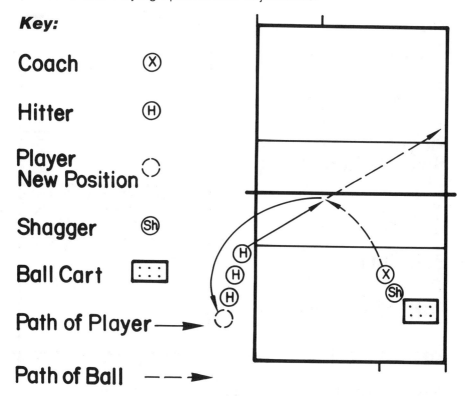

Explanation: The coach positions himself away from the net. There are three hitters per group. The coach tosses the ball to the left front (#4) position, using varying speeds and trajectories. The hitters must adjust the length and speed of their approach to successfully position themselves to spike. After they spike they quickly move to the end of the line. The drill continues for a set number of spikes or set amount of time.

Variations:
1. Run the same drill to the right front (#2) position.
2. Vary the position from which the coach tosses.

Backcourt Attack Drill

Contributor: Bob Bertucci
University of Tennessee

Purpose: To develop the ability to spike from behind the attack line.

Key:

Coach	Ⓧ
Player	◯
Player New Position	◌
Shagger	ⓢʰ
Ball Cart	⬚
Path of Player	⟶
Path of Ball	⤑

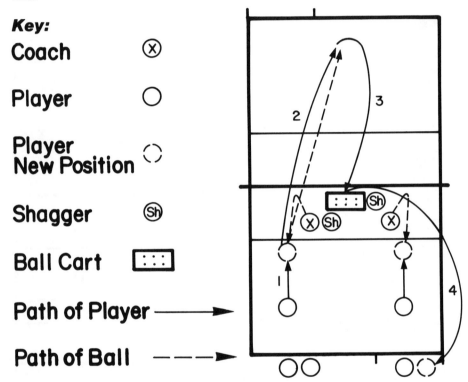

Explanation: Two players begin in backcourt serve reception positions. The coach in the left front (#4) position tosses about 8' deep. The player in the left back (#5) position approaches, jumps behind the attack line, and flies forward to spike the ball to position #5 on the opposite court. Immediately following the hit, the other coach tosses 8' deep to the player in the right back (#1) position who repeats the same movements, spiking to the #1 position on the opposite court. After the players hit, they shag the spiked balls, place them in the carts, and return to the spiking lines.

Variations:
1. Have players hit to different positions.
2. Have players hit from different positions.

Three-Position Hitting Drill

Contributor: Bob Bertucci
University of Tennessee

Purpose: To develop spiking efficiency under pressure; conditioning.

Key:

Hitter	Ⓗ
Tosser	Ⓣ
Player New Position	◯
Shagger	Ⓢⓗ
Chair	h
Ball Cart	⬚
Path of Player	⟶
Path of Ball	− −▶

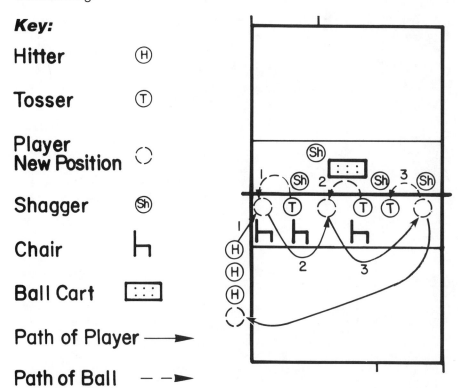

Explanation: The tosser closest to the first hitter tosses a ball to the left front (#4) position. The hitter spikes and immediately runs around the middle chair as the next tosser tosses a ball to the center front (#3) position. The hitter spikes and runs around the last chair as the next tosser tosses a ball to the right front (#2) position. After the third spike, the hitter immediately returns to the left side of the court and continues the circuit.

Variations:
1. Have the hitters spike different sets.
2. Have tossers set balls to the hitters.
3. Use blockers against the spikers.

6

BLOCKING

Blocking Warmup Drill

Contributor: Bob Bertucci
University of Tennessee

Purpose: To develop body control at the net and warming up the body for high intensity work.

Key:

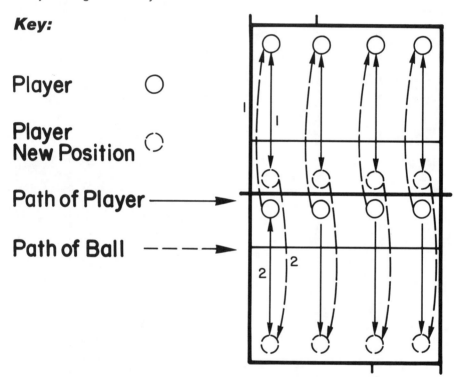

Player   ○

Player
New Position ○

Path of Player ————▶

Path of Ball — — — ▶

Explanation: Four players start at the net with a ball, while four other players start at the baseline. The players at the net start the drill by jumping and tossing the ball to the players at the baseline. The method of tossing simulates the blocking action. The ball is held overhead with two hands and the blocking players, by contracting the abdominal muscles, snap their bodies forward, propelling the ball to their partners. Immediately the tossing players backpedal toward their baseline while their partners are advancing toward the net. The drill is continued for a set number of times.

Variation:
1. The tossing players make the ball bounce at the partner on the baseline.

Continuous Blocking Drill

Contributor: Bob Bertucci
University of Tennessee

Purpose: To practice block footwork and timing.

Key:

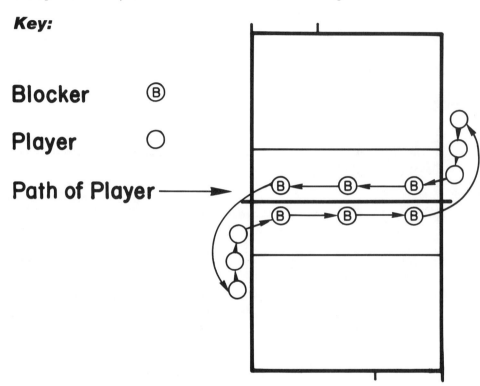

Blocker   Ⓑ

Player   ○

Path of Player ⟶

Explanation: The drill begins with each player jumping and blocking in place. As soon as they land, all players move one blocking position to their right. Players always time their blocks to jump with the players opposite them. After each jump the blockers stepping off the court move to the end of the line on the other side of the net, and a new blocker steps in. Continue for a set time limit.

Variations:
1. Use various types of footwork.
2. Run drill, moving to the left.

Blocking Footwork Drill

Contributor: Bob Bertucci
University of Tennessee

Purpose: To train the step-crossover-hop and step-hop methods of footwork for blocking.

Key:

Blocker   ⒷT

Player
New Position ◯

Path of Player ──────▶

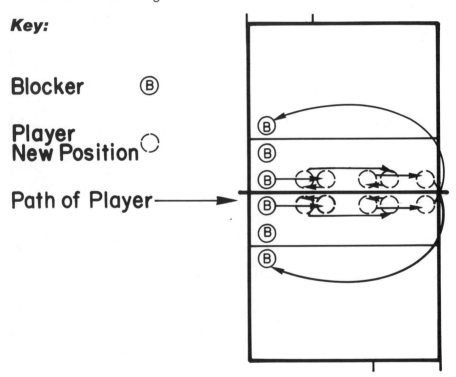

Explanation: The blockers line up on both sides of the net. Beginning at different times, the first blocker starts the drill by executing a standing block. Upon landing, he executes the step-crossover-hop footwork and block. Next, moving in the opposite direction, the player executes a step-hop block. The sequence is repeated until the blocker reaches the opposite side of the court. After completing a full trip, the blocker moves to the end of the opposite line. The drill should be done for a set number of times.

Variation:
1. Have a two-player block during the drill.

Chair Blocking Drill

Contributor: Bob Bertucci
University of Tennessee

Purpose: To develop correct blocking form and footwork.

Key:

Player   ◯

Player
New Position   ◌

Blocker   Ⓑ

Shagger   ⑤ʰ

Chair   ⊓

Ball Cart   ⊡

Path of Player ——▶

Path of Ball — — —▶

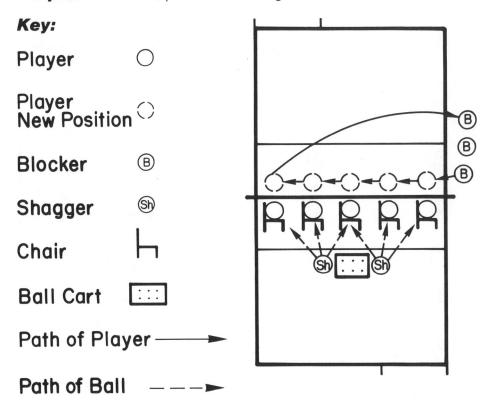

Explanation: Five players stand on chairs on one side of the net. They each hold a ball above the net. The blockers move along the other side of the net, using correct footwork, jumping and penetrating the net to push each ball down, simulating a block. After blocking in each position, move to the end of the line and repeat the drill for a set number of rotations or time. The shaggers near the ball cart feed the players on the chairs.

Variations:
1. Run drill with blockers moving left along the net.
2. The players on the chair can move the ball, forcing the blockers to react.

Rapid Fire Mock Block Drill

Contributor: Bob Bertucci
University of Tennessee

Purpose: To develop correct blocking form, footwork, and timing on the block.

Key:

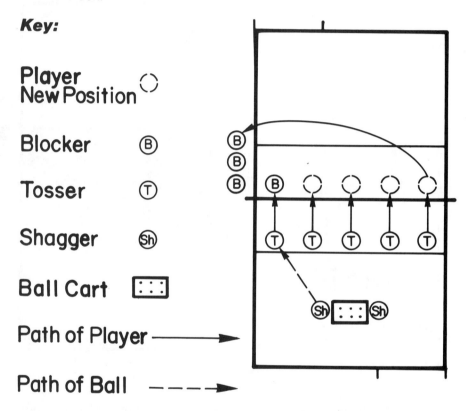

Player
New Position ◯

Blocker Ⓑ

Tosser ⓣ

Shagger ⓢⓗ

Ball Cart ⬚

Path of Player ———➤

Path of Ball – – – ➤

Explanation: Five players start on one side about 8′ away from the net with the ball. The blockers take turns moving along the net, using correct form and footwork, timing the tossed ball and block. The blockers must jump and block each ball as the tossers on the other side throw the balls low over the net.

Variations:
1. Run drill with blockers moving right along the net.
2. Vary the toss slightly to the right or left of the blocker, forcing them to observe and react.

Team Chair Blocking Drill

Contributor: Bob Bertucci
University of Tennessee

Purpose: To develop middle blocker's footwork and the concept of a two-player block.

Key:

Player ⃝

Player New Position ⃝

Blocker Ⓑ

Shagger Ⓢⓗ

Chair ⊢

Ball Cart ⊡

Path of Player ———▶

Path of Ball – – –▶

Explanation: Three players stand on chairs on one side of the net. They each hold a ball above the net. The middle blocker moves to the left, using correct footwork, positions next to the outside blocker and forms a two-player block. This team blocks, jumps and penetrates the net, pushing the ball down, simulating a block. The middle blocker moves to the right, using correct footwork, positions next to the opposite outside blocker, and forms a two-player block. This pair repeats the simulated block. After blocking, the players move to the end of the line. This drill is done for a set number of times.

Variations:
1. Run the drill with the middle blocker moving to the right side first.
2. The players on the chair can move the ball, forcing the blockers to react.
3. The players on the chair can spike the ball instead of holding it.

Watch the Spiker Drill

Contributor: Doug Beal
USA Men's National Team

Purpose: To train the blockers to watch the spiker during the block. Also used to train blocking form.

Key:

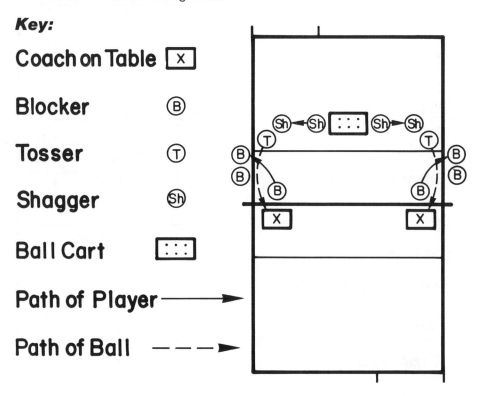

Coach on Table ☐x☐

Blocker Ⓑ

Tosser Ⓣ

Shagger Ⓢⓗ

Ball Cart ⌗⌗⌗

Path of Player ──────▶

Path of Ball ─ ─ ─▶

Explanation: A blocker is situated on the opposite side of the net from the coach. The tosser tosses a ball from behind the blocker to the coach, who spikes. The blocker must watch the coach to get the visual cues needed to block the ball.

Variations:
1. The tosser tosses slightly to the right or left, forcing the blocker to adjust.
2. Use two blockers.

Endurance Blocking

Contributor: Marilyn McReavy
University of Kentucky

Purpose: To emphasize proper movement and blocking skill even as a player experiences fatigue. Works on jumping endurance. Develops determination as well as allows the coach to analyze players' movements and skills easily.

Key:

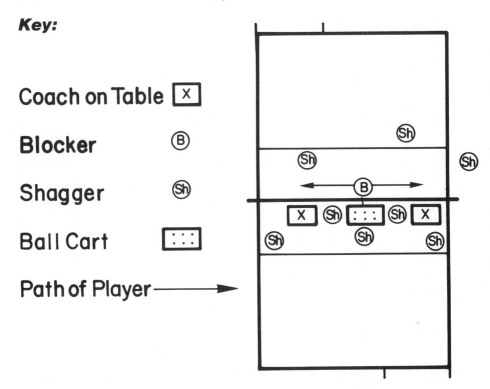

Coach on Table ☒

Blocker Ⓑ

Shagger Ⓢⓗ

Ball Cart ⬚

Path of Player ⟶

Explanation: The blocker moves from one position to the other and attempts to block the ball hit at him. The coach should begin by hitting at the blocker. Emphasize correct footwork. Eliminate incorrect skill even if the drill must go slowly at first. Do not allow bad habits to develop, such as jumping sideways, hitting the net or stepping back from or under the net.

Variations:
1. Use sidestep, turn-and-run, or crossover step.
2. Progress from hitting at the blocker to hitting around or away.

Simple Blocking Drill

Contributor: Bob Bertucci
University of Tennessee

Purpose: To learn to successfully block a spike. To develop footwork and timing for blocking and the concept of a two-player block.

Key:

Coach on Table ☒

Blocker Ⓑ

Player
New Position ⚬

Tosser ⓣ

Shagger ⓢⓗ

Ball Cart ⊡

Path of Player ——➤

Path of Ball — — ➤

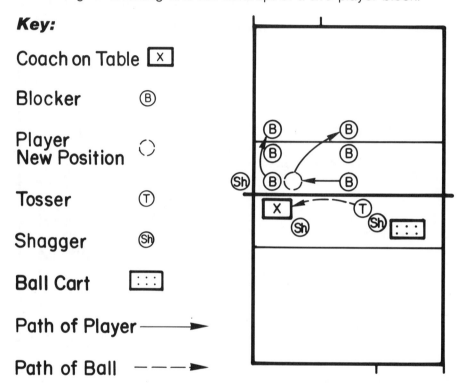

Explanation: One tosser tosses the ball to the coach standing on the table, who in turn spikes directly into the blockers' hands. The middle blocker (#3) moves to the right front (#2) position blocker as soon as the ball is tossed. The blocker in the #2 position positions himself according to the spiker's strongest spiking option. As the middle front (#3) position blocker closes to form the two-player block, both simultaneously leave the floor to intercept the ball. After completing the block, the players return to the end of their line.

Variations:
1. Vary the height of the toss or its distance from the net.
2. Run the same drill to the other side of the net.

Three-Player Technique Blocking Drill

Contributor: Mike Puritz
University of California-Irvine

Purpose: To work on blocking techniques during one-on-one situations and double blocks. Practice footwork, arm, hand and head position. Secondary purpose is for the off blocker to work on movement from the net to the sharp angle position.

Key:

Blocker	Ⓑ
Digger	Ⓓ
Hitter	Ⓗ
Player New Position	◯
Shagger	Ⓢⱨ
Chair	⊢
Ball Cart	⊡
Path of Player	——▶
Path of Ball	— — —▶

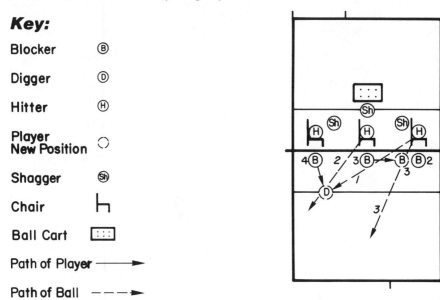

Explanation: The drill starts with three blockers (left #4, middle #3 and right #2) up at the net. Three hitters on chairs are lined up opposite the blockers. The left-side hitter spikes cross court with the #2 blocker working on one-on-one technique. The middle hitter spikes power angle with the #3 blocker blocking one-on-one. Upon landing, blocker #3 uses proper footwork to join blocker #2 as the left-side hitter tries to hit the hole in the block. During step 3, the off blocker (#4) comes off for the sharp angle or dink. The same three steps are performed to the opposite side. Complete a total of six spikes and blocks per set, and six sets per group.

Variations:
1. Adjust chairs for blocking X's, tandems or other combinations.
2. Add additional defenders.

7

DIGGING
& EMERGENCY
TECHNIQUES

Backup Digging Drill

Contributor: Frankie Albitz
Oral Roberts University

Purpose: To teach backpedaling and moving forward on defense.

Key:

Coach   Ⓧ

Digger   Ⓓ

Shagger   Ⓢⓗ

Ball Cart   ⬚

Path of Player   ——→

Path of Ball   ――→

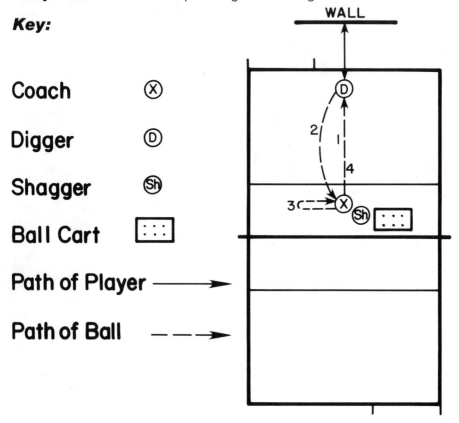

Explanation: One player stands 10′ away with back to the wall. The coach is also 10′ to 15′ from the digger with a ball. The coach spikes the ball at the player who digs it back to the coach. The coach self-sets the ball while the player digging backpedals, touches the wall and runs forward to dig the next spike from the coach. This drill is continuous and should be done for a specific number of digs or amount of time.

Variation:
1. The digger begins facing the wall and, on command, turns, pre-hops and executes the dig.

Coach-Oriented Digging Drill

Contributor: Bob Bertucci
University of Tennessee

Purpose: To practice digging accuracy.

Key:

Coach	Ⓧ
Digger	Ⓓ
Setter/Target	●
Shagger	Ⓢⓗ
Player New Position	◯
Path of Player	——→
Path of Ball	– – –→

Explanation: The coach spikes at the first digger, who passes to the first target. The players rotate clockwise from the digger to target, target to shagger. The first shagger moves to the digging line. Continue the drill for a time limit or a certain number of passes to the target.

Variations:
1. Change the position of the coach.
2. Change the position of the diggers
3. Have the coach stand on a table and hit over the net.

Digger Drill

Contributor: Ralph Hippolyte
Nykoping Volleyball Club, Sweden

Purpose: To teach reading the spiker and digging skills.

Key:

Coach on Table [X]

Digger Ⓓ

Setter/Target ●

Shagger Sʰ

Player
New Position ◯

Ball Cart [⋯]

Path of Player ——→

Path of Ball ––→

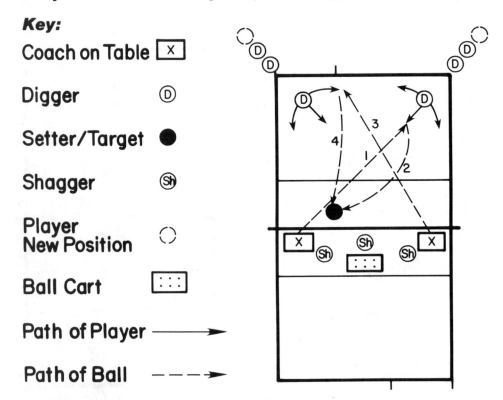

Explanation: The coaches spike cross court to the diggers in their respective corners. Coaches may spike so players must move left, right or forward. Players try to dig balls up to the target. After a digger plays one ball, he returns to the end of the line. Continue until time expires or until a specific number of balls are played to the target. The players must watch the ball in relation to the coaches' body.

Variations:
1. Run the drill down the line or to any area you would start your defensive backcourt players.
2. Add one or two blockers, having the diggers position according to the spiker and blocker.

Go for Two Digging Drill

Contributor: Bob Bertucci
University of Tennessee

Purpose: To develop the ability to play a ball using a dive.

Key:

Coach   (X)

Digger   (D)

Player
New Position   ( )

Shagger   (Sh)

Ball Cart   [:::]

Path of Player   ———→

Path of Ball   – – –→

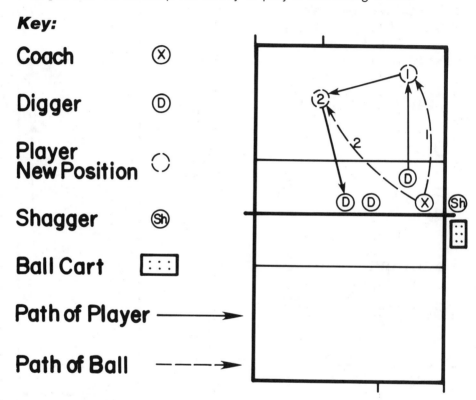

Explanation: The coachs tosses a ball to the left back (#5) position. The first digger must run, dive and attempt to play the ball to the coach. As soon as the first ball is played, the coach tosses another ball to the right back (#1) position, and the same digger again runs, dives, and attempts to play the ball to the coach. The digger then returns to the end of the line. Repeat for a set number of times or amount of time.

Variation:
1. Have players use a roll to play the ball.

Repeat Dig Drill

Contributor: Merri Dwight
Former Head Coach,
Colorado State University

Purpose: To develop individual's defensive positioning, reaction, and reading skills for digging.

Key:

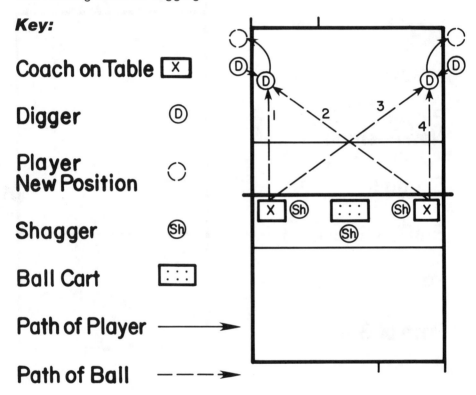

Coach on Table [X]

Digger   Ⓓ

Player
New Position   ◯

Shagger   Ⓢⓗ

Ball Cart   [⋮]

Path of Player   ⟶

Path of Ball   ⇢

Explanation: Two coaches, one in left front (#4) positon, and one in right front (#2) position. Alternate spiking at two diggers. Diggers switch every two balls. The drill continues for specified cycle or time.

Variations:

1. Add blockers.
2. Spike balls, requiring a player to employ an emergency technique for recovery.

Two-2-Minute Defense Drill

Contributor: Kay Woodiel
Arkansas State University

Purpose: To promote readiness on defense, digging skills.

Key:

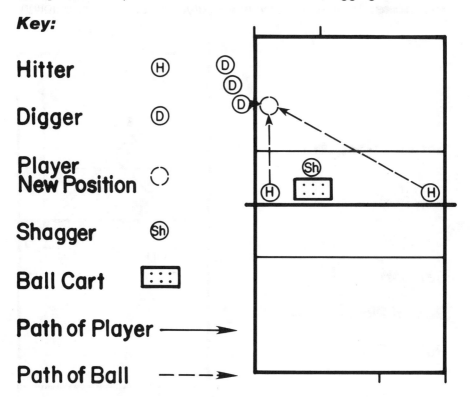

Hitter Ⓗ

Digger Ⓓ

**Player
New Position** ◌

Shagger Ⓢⓗ

Ball Cart ⊡

Path of Player ⟶

Path of Ball --->

Explanation: Start with two hitters on one side of the court located on or outside the sidelines. Each digger moves in one at a time to dig a hit, then returns to the sideline. The hitters alternate attacking line and cross court. Each hitting pair will work for two minutes, changing after one minute.

Variations:
1. Start diggers at the baseline or attack line.
2. Increase difficulty for spike recovery, requiring the players to employ some method of emergency technique.

Position #6 Digger Drill

Contributor: Merri Dwight
Former Head Coach,
Colorado State University

Purpose: To train the middle back player in a player back defense.

Key:

Coach on Table ⊠

Digger Ⓓ

Setter/Target ●

Player
New Position ○

Shagger Ⓢⓗ

Ball Cart ⬚

Path of Player ——→

Path of Ball – – –→

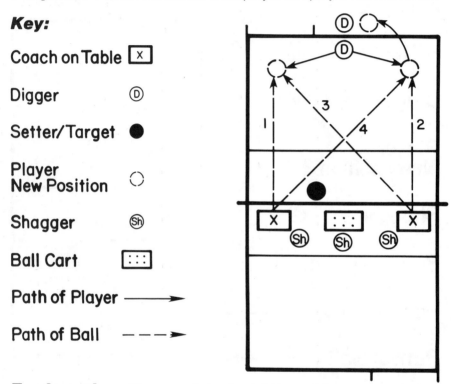

Explanation: The coach in the left front (#4) position spikes down the line. The digger in middle back (#6) position has to move to the right and dig. Immediately after the dig, the coach in the right front (#2) position prepares to spike down the line. The digger has to recover from the first dig and move left to dig the second hit. Again the digger must recover quickly and move right to dig a cross-court spike from the coach in #2 position. The last spike to complete the cycle is a cross-court spike from the coach in the #4 position. After four consecutive digs the player moves to the end of the line. This drill should be done for three complete cycles or a specific amount of time.

Variation:
1. Add blockers so digger learns to dig with a block.

Endurance Digging Drill

Contributor: Kay Johnson
University of North Carolina-Charlotte

Purpose: To dig deep spikes and execute emergency techniques to play short balls; defensive endurance.

Key:

Coach   Ⓧ

Player   ◯

Player
New Position   ◌

Shagger   ⓢⓗ

Ball Cart   ⌗

Path of Player ⟶

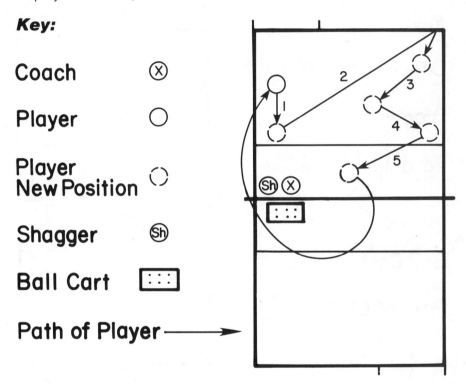

Explanation: Starting from right back (#1) position, the player digs a ball spiked down the line: plays a ball tipped or spiked off the block; moves to left back (#5) position and digs a deep spike; plays a roll shot; digs a ball hit deep toward the sideline; plays a tip. One player repeats the cycle three consecutive times.

Variations:
1. Coach spikes from a table on the other side of the net.
2. Run drill with a group of three players.

Three Back Drill

Contributor: Ed Halik
U.S. Air Force Academy

Purpose: To practice digging, defensive coverage and positioning, conditioning.

Key:

Coach	⊗
Digger	Ⓓ
Target	●
Shagger	ⓢⓗ
Ball Cart	⬚
Path of Ball	– – – →

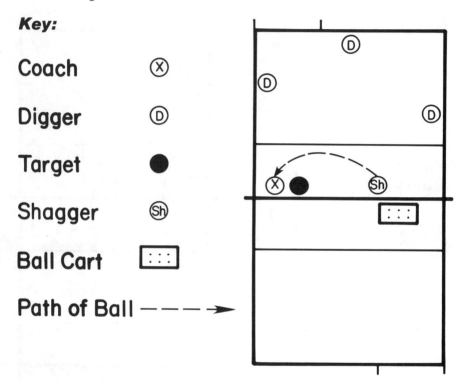

Explanation: A player tosses a ball about 15′ high to the coach. The coach either hits, dinks or roll shots to any position on the court. The defense must play every ball to the target before the next ball is tossed. The same group continues the drill until a particular goal is reached.

Variations:
1. Use different defensive formations.
2. Hit balls directly to beginning players while challenging experienced players.
3. Have coach stand on a table and hit over the net.
4. Have coach hit from different positions.

Left-Side Three-Player Defense Drill

Contributor: John W. Pierce, Jr. Virginia Tech

Purpose: To develop skills, especially protecting seams and open areas of the court.

Key:

Coach	Ⓧ
Digger	Ⓓ
Shagger	Ⓢⱨ
Ball Cart	⊡
Path of Player	⟶
Path of Ball	⤏

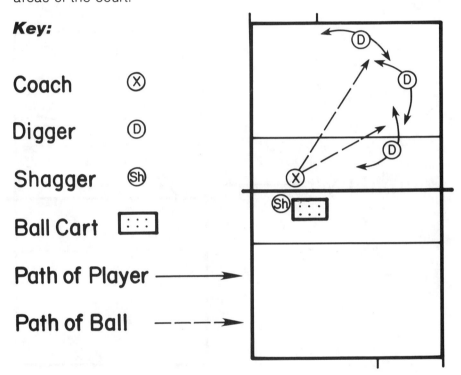

Explanation: Defensive players move to adjust defensive positions on the court. The coach hits balls at the players, who return the ball directly to the coach off the dig. The coach concentrates on seams in defense and open corners.

Variations:
1. Use drill to left or right side.
2. Add a setter in tip receive position who must set all digs to the coach.
3. Use lop shot to line corner, forcing middle back movement.

Four-Player Defense Drill

Contributor: Russ Rose
Penn State University

Purpose: To improve individual defensive skills and team movement in relation to an opponent's attack from various net positions.

Key:

Coach   ⊗

Digger   Ⓓ

Path of Player ────────➤

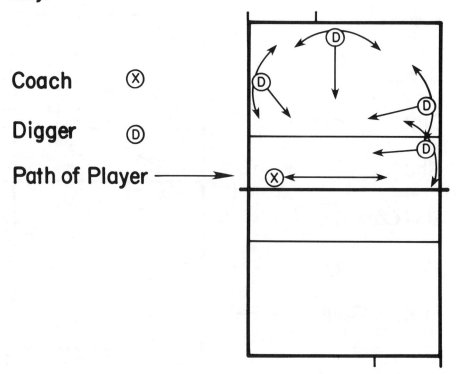

Explanation: The coach hits balls at the players, increasing their range of coverage while emphasizing proper court position. The coach controls the tempo and changes positions along the net to simulate various court positions of an opponent's attack.

Variations:
1. Use different defensive formations.
2. Add a setter to play the second ball to the coach.

Four-Corner Spin Drill

Contributor: Eugenia Kriebel
Butler University

Purpose: This is a good warmup and hustle drill.

Key:

Player   ○

Tosser   Ⓣ

Path of Player ——————▶

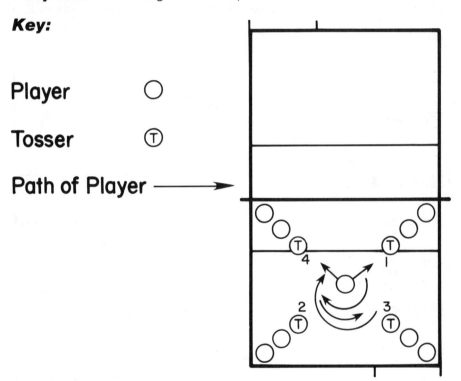

Explanation: The first two players in each line have a ball. One player begins in the center, facing line 1. Tosser #1 throws the ball directly to the middle player. After the pass the middle player must turn to line 2.Tosser #2 throws to the middle player's left, so a roll is necessary. Tosser #3 throws to the middle player's right, and tosser #4 throws short, necessitating a dive. The middle player must recover from each pass and face the next line quickly. On each play the ball should be returned to the tosser. Players may go through one or two times before returning to the end of the line.

Variation:
1. Toss all to one side to stress a specific roll, all short to develop dives, all straight to the player to develop accuracy.

Up and Back Drill

Contributor: Nancy Owen Fortner
Loyola Marymount University

Purpose: To develop physical conditioning, mental conditioning to go to the floor after balls, and to practice emergency techniques.

Key:

Coach   ⊗

Player   ◯

Player
New Position   ♢

Shagger   Ⓢ

Ball Cart   ⌶·∴·⌶

Path of Player ⎯⎯⎯➤

Path of Ball ⎯ ⎯ ⎯➤

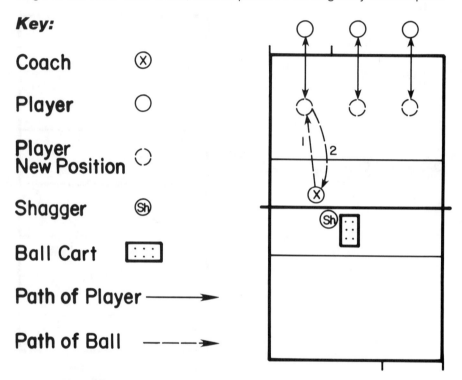

Explanation: Three players start at a position at least 15' to 20' from the endline. Starting with the player on the left side, the coach tosses the ball so the players must execute emergency technique to play the ball. As the first player is recovering to the starting position, the coach tosses to the second player. As the second player is recovering to the starting position, the coach tosses to the third player. Drill continues until group scores + 25.

     + = a good playable dig (can be set).

     0 = a dig that is just touched.

     – = player does not go to floor for the ball and therefore does not
            make an honest effort.

This is a fast pace drill which requires a good shagging system and a large number of balls.

Figure 8 Drill

Contributor: Mario Treibitch
Puerto Rican Women's National Team

Purpose: To increase individual defensive range and vollying as an emergency recovery technique.

Key:

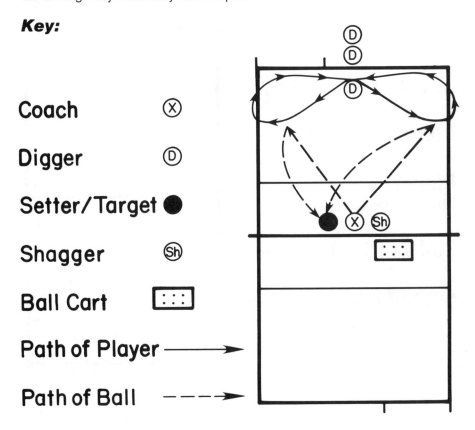

Coach ⊗

Digger Ⓓ

Setter/Target ●

Shagger Ⓢⱨ

Ball Cart ⌷

Path of Player ⟶

Path of Ball ---⟶

Explanation: Players move constantly in a figure 8 pattern to play balls tossed by the coach. All balls should be played to a target. The player moving to play the ball goes inside. The player who has just completed playing the ball goes outside and cuts in over the baseline when center court is reached. This drill should be done till 15 balls are passed to the target.

Variation:
1. The coach spikes the ball instead of tossing.

Net Recovery Drill

Contributor: Amanda Burk
University of Idaho

Purpose: To practice playing a ball out of the net, improve reaction and concentration.

Key:

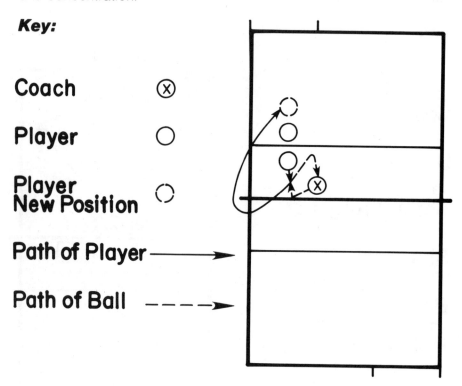

Coach	⊗
Player	○
Player New Position	◌
Path of Player	—————▶
Path of Ball	– – – –▶

Explanation: The coach stands several feet from the net and hits the ball into the net. A single line of players moves one after the other to play the netted ball and forearm-passes the ball back up to the coach. who again hits the ball into the net for the next person to recover. One ball is kept in play as long as possible. If the ball is not kept in play the player retrieves the loose ball and places it on the coach's hip until needed.

Variation:
1. have the players' line situated in different positions at the net.

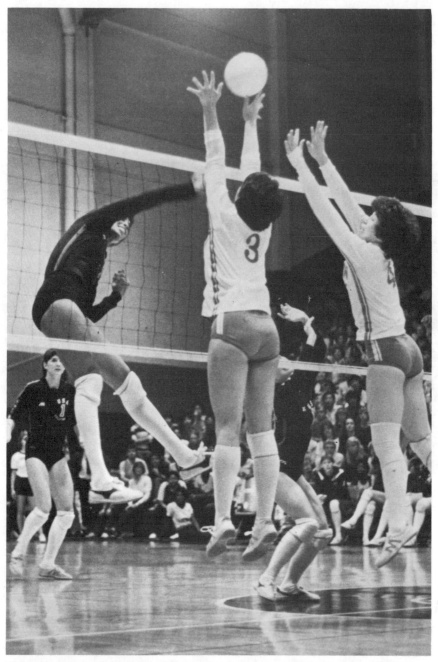

FLO HYMAN, clearly the world's dominant female volleyball player, delivers a spike in a recent match against Japan. Impressive on both offense and defense, the 6'5" Flo has been a member of the USA Women's National Volleyball Team since 1975.